W9-BIE-093

JAKUSHO KWONG

EDITED BY PETER LEVITT

HARMONY BOOKS, NEW YORK

No Beginning, No End

The Intimate Heart of Zen

Copyright © 2003 by Jakusho Kwong

All rights reserved. No part of this book may be reproduced or transmitted in any form or by any means, electronic or mechanical, including photocopying, recording, or by any information storage and retrieval system, without permission in writing from the publisher.

Published by Harmony Books, New York, New York.
Member of the Crown Publishing Group, a division of Random House, Inc.

www.randomhouse.com

Harmony Books is a registered trademark and the Harmony Books colophon is a trademark of Random House, Inc.

Printed in the United States of America

Calligraphy by Jakusho Kwong

Design by Lauren Dong

Library of Congress Cataloging-in-Publication Data
Kwong, Jakusho.
   No beginning, no end : the intimate heart of Zen / Jakusho Kwong.
1. Spiritual life—Zen Buddhism.   I. Title.
 BQ9288 . K86167   2003
 294.3'444—dc21   2002012237

ISBN 0-609-61080-5

10 9 8 7 6 5 4 3 2

First Edition

Dedicated to Shunryu Suzuki-roshi
and all the myriad streams
appearing and disappearing
that constantly
flow to the ocean

may this one drop be a cure
for universal sickness

CONTENTS

ACKNOWLEDGMENTS 9

FOREWORD BY THICH NHAT HANH 13

INTRODUCTION BY PETER LEVITT 15

Coming Alive

1 ONE INCH SITTING, ONE INCH BUDDHA 25

2 FROST GATHERING ON SNOW 32

3 HALF MOON MAKES FULL HALO 36

4 THE ART OF RECEIVING 39

5 RENUNCIATION 44

6 BUDDHA'S LIFE-GIVING PRECEPTS 50

7 YOUR TEACHER IS FOUND IN YOUR PRACTICE 53

8 SPIRIT OF COOKING 61

9 BREAKING THE SKIN BORN OF MOTHER 65

10 TWO SCHOOLS, ONE SAMADHI 73

11 THE SOUND OF THE BELL 79

12 CONFIDENCE IN YOUR ORIGINAL NATURE 84

13 LIFE OF VOW: GOING STRAIGHT ON A
   NINETY-NINE-MILE CURVE 93

14 LEAVES FALL 102

the Treasure

15 INTIMATE STUDY 111

16 TAKING THE BACKWARD STEP 119

17 ACTIVE PARTICIPATION IN LOSS 128

18 DIAMOND AND COAL, THE PURE HEART OF PRACTICE 139

19 YOU CAN'T GET OFF THE TRAIN 149

20 THE RIVER LONGS TO RETURN TO THE OCEAN 162

21 FINDING OURSELVES JUST AS WE ARE 169

22 DOING FOR THE THING ITSELF 175

As It Is

23 SONOMAMA 185

24 A LOTUS IN YOUR GARDEN 192

25 THINGS AS IT IS 195

26 THE DEAD FAWN 203

27 SHIKAN TAZA: SITTING QUIETLY AND DOING NOTHING 207

28 PLUM BLOSSOMS 219

29 THE WORDLESS PROCLAMATION 225

30 TURNING YOUR RADIANCE INWARD 234

APPENDIX: TEN CHARACTERISTICS OF OUR INCONCEIVABLY WONDROUS NATURE 251

ACKNOWLEDGMENTS

IN THE EARLY SPRING of 1984 I returned to Tassajara, the Zen monastery near Big Sur founded by my teacher, Suzuki-roshi. I went there with a few of my students for the purpose of bringing several large stones, each weighing up to two tons, from Tassajara Creek to our temple on Sonoma Mountain. I wanted to create a memorial stone, a stupa, dedicated to Suzuki-roshi. The date chosen for the ceremony to place Roshi's relics and ashes at the stupa was April 29. It turned out to be a very auspicious date. On that same date years earlier Roshi's ashes had been scattered at Tassajara in the midst of a great windstorm that blew in from Big Sur—a storm so fierce that it almost knocked us down. This was also the same date that Mitsu Suzuki's first husband was shot down in his plane over China during World War II. In her letters to him, she had said, "Don't bomb the Chinese. They are just like us." When I told Mitsu-sama (who later became Suzuki-roshi's wife) about the date, she wept.

April 29, 1984, was a calm day on Sonoma Mountain, but during the ceremony we suddenly felt a strong gust of wind, so strong that Suzuki-roshi's son, Hoitsu Suzuki, looked up and acknowledged that Suzuki-roshi usually appears in the form of wind. I felt his presence that day just as I have felt it so many other times in my life. And even now I feel it in acknowledging that it was his wisdom and compassion that led me to practice and live on Sonoma Mountain from 1973 until today, to give many Dharma talks and eventually to write this book.

It was my good karma to have met Suzuki-roshi in San Francisco in the spring of 1960 and to have been with him even for the brief period of eleven years before he died. I acknowledge with deepest gratitude his influence and that of three other Zen teachers on my early being: Dainin Katagiri-roshi, Kobun Chino Otogawa-roshi, and Hoitsu Suzuki-roshi. They, together with many other teachers including Maezumi-roshi, Uchiyama-roshi, Zen master Seung Sahn, Mahaghosananda, His Holiness the XIV Dalai Lama, Thich Nhat Hanh, Chögyam Trungpa Rinpoche, and Mrs. Mitsu Suzuki-sensei, represent the spirit that is behind the words in this book.

No Beginning, No End is based on talks given over a twenty-seven-year period on Sonoma Mountain and also over the past fourteen years at Kannon Sangha in Poland and Natthagi (Night Pasture) Sangha in Iceland. It represents a kind of harvest of Dharma work over the many seasons. (The metaphor is quite apt since we actually did have a vineyard on Sonoma Mountain during our first thirteen years.)

I express my deep appreciation to all the members of these sanghas who listened to the talks, asked questions, recorded the audiotapes, and made careful transcriptions of so many words, especially Mikolaj Markiewicz, Jerzy Dmuchowski, Ewa Orlowska, Helga Joakimsdottir, and Oskar Ingolfsson. It was through the work of the people doing the audiotape recordings that I learned to appreciate that beautiful pause between the changing of tapes!

Chris King, the longtime editor of our newsletter, Mountain

Wind, and Neil Meyers spent many hours verifying quoted material and checking references. Carol Lingman offered helpful suggestions at key points in the book's development and attended to small details with great care. Demian Kwong coordinated the ever-present and often-tedious details of communication and office support with diligence and patient effort. Early on Royce Latham left the imprint of "high resolution" in reproducing the original works of calligraphy to the very end with constancy. I am greatly indebted to Ron Champoux for his invaluable professional assistance at a critical point in the book's evolution. The generosity of these and many unnamed *sangha* members supported the publication of this work. And especially an anonymous donor.

Sojun Mel Weitsman-roshi and Michael Wenger-roshi from the San Francisco Zen Center were gracious and unhesitating in their support for the use of quotes from Suzuki-roshi. Bill Redican, the SFZC archivist, gave ready assistance in tracking some source material from Suzuki-roshi's unpublished talks.

Linda Loewenthal, my editor at Harmony Books, was sensitive enough to recognize and understand the value of making this book available and accessible to an audience far beyond the Zen community. Her encouragement was very inspiring, and I feel it is my good fortune this work found its way to her. I am grateful to our agent, Anne Edelstein, for making this connection with all of us possible.

It is impossible to adequately acknowledge the contribution made by my wife and senior student, Laura Shinko, not just in the creation of this book but as a partner, practitioner, and cofounder in my life's work. Her unusual dedication, compassion, selflessness, courage, and devotion to the Dharma—risking unpredictable energy—has also showed me the way by always being there. I also want to express my love and gratitude to our sons: Ryokan, Cam, Evri, and Demian, who in their unseen ways helped and supported us throughout our journey.

I am grateful to Peter Levitt, who first proposed the idea of creating a book and who persevered in the face of more than sixteen hundred pages of typescript. With his insight and his long experience as a poet and writer, Peter did a wonderful job of editing, organizing, and shaping the material for this book. He was able to convey the voice of the teaching as true to its content as possible. I'm also grateful to Peter's wife, Shirley Graham, for the time generously given during the three years of this book's creation.

Again, I would like to acknowledge all the beings here and abroad who have come to practice on Sonoma Mountain and have in many varied and mysterious ways helped me in study and practice over the endless seasons of this continuous practice-lineage of Suzuki-roshi.

—JAKUSHO KWONG

Foreword

IT HAS BEEN SAID that the twenty-first century is going to be a century of spirituality. If it is not a century of spirituality, there will be very difficult times ahead for all of us and for the generations to come. If we are not able to stop and look more deeply at the suffering in ourselves, how will we be able to address the suffering in the world around us? In order for us to transform our own suffering, we must do something radical.

The first radical thing we can do to transform the suffering in ourselves is to practice stopping *(shamatha)*. We stop in order to return to ourselves, to become calm. When we are calm, we have a better chance to see our suffering more clearly. The second radical act is to look deeply inside ourselves and see our suffering, be with our suffering, in order to understand and transform it. This is also true for the suffering in the world. We as entire nations need to *stop* and look deeply at the suffering in the world in order to see it more clearly without prejudice and understand how to transform it.

The practice of mindfulness in these troubled times is more important than ever. If we as individuals do not take the time to practice mindfulness, not only will it be difficult to transform the suffering in our own lives, but it will be difficult to transform the suffering in the world. It is vital to ourselves, our children, and the Earth that we have a practice that helps us to be mindful, that lets us come back to ourselves and dwell in the present moment in order to transform suffering in ourselves and others around us.

The easiest way for anyone to practice mindfulness is to join a *sangha*. When we come together as a *sangha*, we support each other in the practice, and what may seem difficult to do by ourselves at home becomes natural and enjoyable with Dharma friends. The energy of a true *sangha*, a *sangha* that has acceptance, understanding, compassion, and love, is great enough to sustain and nourish all its members and support them in transforming their suffering to joy, peace, and compassion.

To have a loving teacher who supports the *sangha* in this important work of transformation is a rare and wonderful gift. In the spirit of a true student, Jakusho Kwong shows his love and respect for his teachers and the appreciation he has for the teachings he has received from them. And in the spirit of a genuine teacher, Jakusho Kwong wholeheartedly shares these gifts with his *sangha* and all of us.

—*THICH NHAT HANH*
Plum Village, France

INTRODUCTION

YEARS AGO, during a break in the schedule at Sonoma Mountain Zen Center, I wrote a short poem on a slip of paper, and later in the day, when we had all gathered for a snack in the *sangha* house, I handed the poem to Roshi. He looked at it and without a word went to the bulletin board and posted the unsigned poem with a push pin. The poem was as follows:

> *Jakusho's shaved head*
> *just like a fish—*
> *hard to grasp from outside*

Then he and I stood beside each other awaiting our turn to take tea from the teapot that was set on the table just to the right of the bulletin board. All this time, though we stood only inches apart, we did not exchange so much as a glance or say a word.

As Roshi was pouring his tea, another student who was now standing before the bulletin board reading the day's notes suddenly burst into laughter and turned to Roshi while pointing to the poem. "That's great!" he said. "Who wrote it?" Roshi continued pouring with his characteristic care and did not break his concentration for a moment. Then as he stood with his head bowed over his cup, I heard him answer softly, "Someone very close to me."

In the early thirteenth century Eihei Dogen, the founder of Soto Zen, said that enlightenment is just intimacy with all things. Jakusho's shaved head may be hard to grasp from the outside, but so is our Buddha Nature. In fact, to realize our own true nature from the outside is impossible. Whether in word or deed, Jakusho Kwong-roshi's teachings make this clear in every way. He will sometimes use a shout, sometimes his *roshi's* stick struck against the *zendo* floor, and sometimes a voice so soft and a meaning so subtle in its profundity or sly humor that one learns to stay alert in order not to miss a thing. Of course, this is exactly what he wants for us, since each of these skillful means is meant to point us in the direction of ourselves, the only place where intimacy with all things is possible. Then, not only can Jakusho's shaved head be "grasped," but no grasping is necessary at all, which is what Roshi teaches time and time again: Why grasp for what is already here?

This is an intimate book. It is a mind reaching out to touch itself for the benefit of others, a heart that tells the reader, "I want to convey to you the most important thing," a life lived in such a way that this vow may actually be accomplished. In each of these chapters the intimate presence of Kwong-roshi's voice and teachings seem to rise from the ground of his own considerable intuition directly into that of the reader in a kind of uninterrupted mind-to-mind transmission that takes place beyond words, which is a signature of Zen expression. And so, in the end, the reader experiences these teachings as the kind, modest, unadorned voice of his or her own wise heart. The heart of the reader, the teacher, the Buddha, all one.

Jakusho Kwong-roshi has spent years seeing into the heart of our human situation. He knows that in essence he is no different from anyone else, and so he knows that we, like all people at all times, yearn to return to the state of wholeness that is our birthright. From a Zen perspective, our wholeness is always right here, though our own misunderstanding may prevent us from realizing this simple truth. That this yearning is part of what it means to be a human being—in fact, the very part that most often brings people to spiritual practice—is never far from his mind. This is why he has offered these teachings in the spirit of his friend Allen Ginsberg's poem "Song," which ends with the lines:

> *yes, yes,*
> > *that's what*
> *I wanted,*
> > *I always wanted,*
> *I always wanted,*
> > *to return*
> *to my body*
> > *where I was born*

But Kwong-roshi also knows that to be able to accomplish this return, this coming back to where we were born, or *are* born moment after moment as he reminds us throughout this book, we must live according to a particular understanding of the word *intimacy.* This was taught to him and cultivated in him by his beloved teacher, Shunryu Suzuki-roshi, who began preparing him to be one of only two American disciples to receive direct transmission so that he could carry the lineage, and teachings, further into the heart of America as his Dharma heir—a process that Suzuki-roshi's death would interrupt.

Suzuki-roshi taught that real intimacy means *through and through;* a way of living our daily lives, rooted in the practice of Zen, so that everything is included in what we do, and yet we leave no trace. When we live with this kind of intimacy, we are always expressing our true self, the wholeness of our original nature, which has neither beginning nor end.

True Zen masters live *through and through.* You can see it in the way they pour tea, place their shoes together outside the meditation hall, walk down the road. You can feel the presence of their intimacy with all things in their undivided way of engaging in any activity their daily lives may bring. There is a vitality in their manner of speaking and in their gestures, no matter how small, that makes it seem that the whole of life has just entered the room. And it has. Jakusho Kwong-roshi says this is Zen. It is not something special, to be found exclusively in the meditation hall, but rather it is the aliveness we bring to our everyday lives, the aliveness that is already present within us waiting to emerge.

Kwong-roshi, whose singular and beautiful calligraphy is included on the pages of this book, has a unique way of presenting his Dharma. He sketches intuitively with words. He has complete confidence in what he calls the *basic goodness* of our nature and in the absolute interconnectedness, the Oneness, of all beings. He knows, and reminds readers again and again, that what he expresses in his teachings is really just the contents of our own hearts and minds, if only we will see it. In order to help this seeing and understanding to occur, he presents his teachings in a manner that is as natural to him as breathing, one that appeals to our deep minds with its poetic intuition and yet is one hundred percent pragmatic and meant to be used, like a beautifully glazed cup for drinking tea, or a rake whose natural polish has emerged from years of contact between a human hand and the slender wood.

In editing this book I have done my best to preserve Kwong-roshi's spontaneous and intimate expression so that his presence may be felt on every page. Therefore, readers should not think they are going to hear a Zen master speak to them from a distance. Kwong-roshi speaks from close up, very close. As he says about his teacher, Suzuki-roshi, his talks transmit the most intimate thing to us in an ordinary way—so ordinary that readers may hear it as their own heart and mind, which is the heart and mind of the Buddha. As it says in the classic Zen motto: Your ordinary mind, that is the Way.

In many of the chapters of this book, which is divided into three parts, "Coming Alive," "The Treasure," and "As It Is," Kwong-roshi weaves into his teaching stories from the considerable literature of Zen that are not as well known as some but that are moving, accessible, and true. Then he offers his unique and inspiring understanding, which has been cultivated by more than forty years of daily *zazen*. In addition he relates modern stories from our time in which other contemporary teachers appear, including His Holiness the Dalai Lama, Thich Nhat Hanh, Maezumi-roshi, Zen master Seung Sahn, Katagiri-roshi, and others. This is his way of "sharing the stage," so to speak, so that the wisdom and compassion of these fine teachers may help us to find meaning and express our true selves in even the smallest act of our everyday lives.

And then there is Shunryu Suzuki-roshi, whose profound understanding, distilled expression, and powerful presence is felt, and heard, throughout this book. We meet him in both previously unpublished teachings of Suzuki-roshi's, which Kwong-roshi has always offered as part of the fabric of his own teaching, and anecdotal glimpses of Jakusho Kwong's early days with his teacher as Suzuki-roshi helped to cultivate his young disciple's understanding. These latter are alternately so moving and so downright funny, I hope the reader will consider them a hidden treasure of the book.

In closing I would like to offer the following observation. Traditionally the face of Zen has been portrayed either as stern or as mysterious and enigmatic and therefore inaccessible. Often it has been presented in a romantic yet almost inhuman light as its practitioners appear in one tale after another applying themselves to its rigorous demands. In truth, these attributions to Zen have been found quite attractive by some and forbidding or distancing by others. "What is this Zen business?" they ask. "It appeals to me, but I don't get it." (Those who say "I don't get it" are actually closer to Zen than they may suspect.) In recent years the advertising industry has even begun using the word *Zen* to imply certain inexpressible qualities to their products with the hope of enticing new customers to buy either Zen This or Zen That. But Kwong-roshi holds up no such billboards and makes no promises on the subject of Zen. His teachings and the stories he tells serve to demystify both Zen and our lives, and I believe they do so with refreshing honesty, humility, and humor. To this end he is not in any way shy of using his own human story, including the struggles, mistakes, and misunderstandings he had to endure along the way. This is his way of holding up a generous mirror in which the reader may see a face he or she recognizes as their own. After all, his only goal has been to help his companions along the road to discover the treasure of their own lives right where they are, moment after moment, time and time again. He will use anything at hand to help that come about.

I would like to end with a story about the beginning. As he tells it, the first time Jakusho met Shunryu Suzuki-roshi, the man who was to become his teacher, he was twenty-five years old and had wandered in to Soko-ji, a Japanese Buddhist temple in San Francisco "to see what was going on. It was 1960," Jakusho says, "beatnik time, and I just walked into the meditation hall with my boots on to have a look around. Then I saw someone enter through a door at the opposite end of the hall. Of course, I didn't know it at the time, but it was Suzuki-roshi. Though I knew we could see each other, I didn't look at him, and he didn't look at me. I didn't look at him because I had been watching a lot of samurai movies and felt I was very cool, and he didn't look at me because he was a Zen master.

"As I watched he walked directly to the altar, and with a great deal of care, began to rearrange some flowers that were standing on the altar in a tall vase. When I saw this I thought, 'This is Square Zen,' and I walked out. But sometime later I came to realize that because he was a Zen master and gave one hundred percent of himself to rearranging those flowers, as he did to everything, in that moment he was actually rearranging my mind."

—PETER LEVITT
Salt Spring Island,
British Columbia

One Inch Sitting, One Inch Buddha

When the sun first comes up and shines on you, he said, your shadow is big behind you. But as you continue to sit, your shadow gets smaller and smaller, until finally it's just Buddha sitting there.

IN THE EARLY 1960S, at the Zen Center in San Francisco (which was also known as Soko-ji), there was a Buddhist priest from Japan who became discouraged because he couldn't speak English very well. He felt so badly about this that he was thinking of giving up and returning to his country. He told this to Suzuki-roshi, who responded by inviting the priest to a talk he was giving the next day. But during his lecture Suzuki-roshi used only a total of about twelve English words. He started off with something like, "Today is today." And then he said something in Japanese. Then he said, "Today is not tomorrow." And he followed that with something in Japanese again. Then he said, "Today is absolutely today." And so on. But all the time he was expressing himself with complete confidence from a presence beyond our thinking, conceptually limited mind.

If you come to listen to a talk as if you are going to hear something great from somebody else, this is a big mistake. The word *teisho* means something you already intimately know, and it is during the *teisho* that the roshi makes the Dharma, or truth, come alive. So the Dharma talk is really going on twenty-four hours a day. Sometimes it seems like it's with Roshi. Sometimes it's with the sound of an airplane. Sometimes it's with the heater turning on. Sometimes it's with roosters crowing across the way or the sound of wind and rain on a corrugated metal roof. But the Dharma talk is going on continuously, without interruption, realized or not. We should remember this. It's usually very near at hand, preciously close, and always with you.

During a recent visit Hoitsu Suzuki-roshi, Suzuki-roshi's son and a very good teacher and friend of ours here at Sonoma Mountain, was describing a calligraphy he did. A rough translation of the calligraphy is "One inch sit. One inch Buddha." It's interesting to note that the word *Buddha* comes from the Sanskrit syllable *budd,* which means "awakened." When he showed us the calligraphy, he mentioned that it had to do with shadow and light. When the sun first comes up and shines on you, he said, your shadow is big behind you. But as you continue to sit, your shadow gets smaller and smaller, until finally it's just Buddha sitting there. Just the sitting Buddha. You are exactly the same as the sitting Buddha.

Our sitting style is called "silent illumination," but just because it's *silent* doesn't mean that nothing is happening. Or said another way, literally Nothing *is* happening! This illumination shines throughout your body, breath, and mind and dissolves your delusions based on greed, anger, and ignorance. And that's exactly how the light and the dark interact. In the case of sound—for instance, when the heater turns on or a cell phone rings—the ears hear the sound and an interaction takes place. Just as it does when I strike my stick on the floor: *Bam!* And though, again, it is beyond our thinking or conceptual mind, there is an intimate communication here. This is *Nothing is happening.* No one can pinpoint exactly what, or where, or when. As you sit, you'll discover this for yourself, and you'll also discover that through your sitting practice you will develop some kind of stability in your life. There's something very deep and immovable in yourself that was always there, just like right now there are some buds on the trees and plants, little ones. And if you were to look, even in the deep snow you'd discover some small sprouts already growing.

There's a Japanese word, *anshin,* that is very important for us to understand. Basically it means "calm, serene, undisturbed." But its meaning also reaches much further than those words. *Anshin* implies that the question of the self has been settled. The question of life and death has been resolved, and your spiritual question has been fulfilled. That's true liberation. Even to translate it as "calm and serene" doesn't quite touch it, because these words actually refer to their *source,* the empty essence from which the whole universe springs forth.

One way to express this idea is to say that this "something," which is so deep, immovable, and pervasive, always lies within you just like an unseen sprout in the snow. Small as it is, in time this sprout will stand as a whole tree. And of course, since it is rooted in *anshin,* as the sprout grows, we naturally come into our own presence at the same time.

Suzuki-roshi's temple in Japan, Rinso-in, is a five-hundred-year-old temple with a mountain behind and a valley below. Through the trees on the temple grounds you can see glimpses of Suruga Bay. When Suzuki-roshi came to America in December 1959, he had to leave many, many people, actually hundreds of people, because Rinso-in is a mother temple to many other temples. In general we don't easily understand people leaving something they love and treasure to do something they feel they must do. When Hoitsu became the abbot of the temple after his father left, he was very young. He may have been in his early thirties. Some of the people it served were ninety years old, and Hoitsu was three times younger than some of the members of the *sangha*. Needless to say, it was a little daunting. He was confronted with how to perform the ceremonies for four or five funerals on a winter day, one after the other, or how to meet with elders of the temple who were seventy to eighty years old. It wasn't easy, but while Suzuki-roshi was over here, Hoitsu had to do it. It was like being thrown into the lion's den. But isn't each one of us also thrown into this life where it's either sink or swim? What will help us float? That's what we want to know, even though sometimes we need to sink a little bit. Sometimes we may sink a lot, and sometimes we may even touch the bottom. *Bam!* But touching the bottom makes for change.

One day an old woman came to Hoitsu for advice. During their discussion she said, "When I die, I'd like you to sing a song for me." Hoitsu was surprised and maybe even a little afraid, because the song the old woman requested was a pop song. He didn't know what to do, so he said, "I cannot do it because I don't feel comfortable. I'm not ready to sing a pop song at a funeral." Usually at funerals the priest wears red robes and leads a formal ritual, but since that was her request, he said to her, "In ten years when you die, I can sing the song, and when I do, I'll sing it from the bottom of my heart."

That decision may have made the woman's life ten years longer, because she had to wait. It also made Hoitsu ten years stronger, because he made a promise. So in this way we give life to each other, and the life we give is based on something. It's like being in a *sangha*. One way to understand what *sangha* means is that it's like stones rubbing against each other until they all become smooth. Zen is not about being nice. We don't strive to be nice people, because we already are. We should know this, even though some of us who are studying Zen have become nice people and do good things. But we do rub up against each other. That's real intimacy, real respect, real compassion for one another. *Sangha* life is just like a pearl; there's much rubbing, and the more agitation there is, the more pearl-like our lives become.

Since Zen came to the West from Japan, it's somewhat easy to confuse what is culturally Japanese with what is Zen. There's been quite a bit of discussion about this issue in recent years. One thing that is clear is that it's important that we don't become Japanese but that we become American or Polish or Icelandic or whatever we happen to be. In my own case, because I studied as a young man at the Zen Center with Suzuki-roshi for many years, I identified with him and wanted to become Japanese. One day he came to me and said, "You're Chinese. You should remember that." And I said, *"Hai!"* just as a Japanese person would. But that's the Japanese style. It's a very good style. It means "I'm open to it. I'm willing, without hesitation." But here in the West we have to adapt it. We have to find a way to express what's inside that *Hai!* Yes!

When the meal is served in the dining hall at the Sixth Ancestor's temple in Shaoguan, China, the woman who cooks the food comes out from the kitchen and says, "My meal is not very good food. I'm sorry." In the West we come out and say, "My meal is great. I hope you like it." But somewhere in between there is a way. As the East meets the West, the way these two come together is very important. Just like the great historian, the late Arnold Toynbee, said, one of the most important things in the twentieth century is the Buddhadharma coming west because of its approach to mind. *What is it?* is the eternal question. This is its greatest gift, and we have been given the gift of having an opportunity to fathom it and use it to help others.

Maezumi-roshi was the founder of Zen Center of Los Angeles and a significant person in the transmission of Zen to the West. After he died, I was given the opportunity to participate in the funeral ceremony by being the person who formally answers the questions in the auditorium. And so without hesitation I said "Yes!" to Bernie Glassman-roshi, who had offered me this opportunity, even though afterward my heart was almost in my mouth. But what else could I say; it was going to be Maezumi-roshi's funeral! So I said, "Yes!" My duties included sitting in front of eight hundred people to answer questions, and the first person to ask a question would be his daughter, Michi. What would I say?

Before the ceremony started, a group of us met in Maezumi-roshi's house. His younger brother, Junyu-roshi, who considered Maezumi his teacher, was there, and he sat at one end of a very long table talking with Bernie Glassman-roshi. I was sitting with my wife Shinko and some others at the other end of the table. It was a very hot day, and we were all being served some cold beer. Without any introduction all of a sudden Junyu-roshi leaned over the table, looked at me with a smile, and said, "How long can you live?" Because of the circumstances of how far away we seemed to be sitting from each other, and people talking, and the heat of the day, I didn't feel that I heard exactly what he said, though I strained to hear the words coming from his direction. I became aware that all of a sudden things seemed very slow, almost like in a dream, so I leaned forward and said, "Do you mean that you're asking me how long can I live?" Now there was a great silence at the table, and everything stopped. Then, lucky thing, I had a glass of beer in my hand. I stood up, walked over to him, leaned in, and *clink,* that was it! This was a spontaneous response just before Maezumi-roshi's funeral ceremony. Or perhaps I should say, the funeral had already begun.

2

Frost Gathering on Snow

We all know how small an individual snowflake is, but
as these individual snowflakes gather together and frost
begins to spread, it is actually transmission of Dharma, of
Truth, and pretty soon you can see one whole mountain.

ACH TIME I SIT before you, I want to convey the most
important thing. I want people to experience this greatness, this vastness, what may be called this *mysterious uni-*
verse that, without doubt, is within each one of us. It's pretty hard
to describe, but when we use a phrase like "cultivate your own
spirit," the word *spirit* includes the whole universe, and this is
what I want to share, with the hope that people may experience
it for themselves. But it is not so easy to do.

This brings to mind something His Holiness the Fourteenth
Dalai Lama said: If you look for a teacher, you should really be
very, very suspicious of the possible teacher and not take what
he or she says for granted. When we look for a teacher, he
stressed, we must test them. Actually, it is very common in the
Dharma, and a real strong point, to think of Dharma as something we should test. *Dharma* refers both to truth and to the

Buddha's teachings. So even though I have this hope to be able to convey the universe to you, what I can really do is to invite each of you to practice, so that you may find it as your own treasure, which is always with you.

It may be that there's some gold under this *zendo,* a great amount of raw gold, but first we have to know that there's gold somewhere in order to begin to look for it, and when we find it, we have to be the ones who extract it. We have to be the ones who take it out. Actually that's a treasure in itself. It's quite useless if the gold stays in the ground, or if the treasure stays within yourself without your ever finding it. That's why I invite you to participate in discovering your own gold. Just reading about Zen, or listening to Dharma talks, is not enough. But it is enough when you find the treasure and experience it for yourself. Then you can discover that it's true and give it away to everyone.

Recently my wife Shinko and I were at Salt Point on the Sonoma County coast. We came upon this very beautiful part of the ocean, which we had heard about for many years, and it turned out that what we heard was really true. It wasn't just the beauty of this place that was so powerful. There seemed to be a special energy in the rocks along the area of the shoreline that could really be felt. Once we passed Salt Point, the energy was gone, and we couldn't help but wonder, "Why is it there and not here?"

This particular lookout point is one where people go to watch whales. On the sign that describes the lookout it says that a whale swims according to the rhythm of its breath. For almost every exhalation, the whale travels a few hundred feet. But on the third or fourth exhalation it goes one thousand feet! It's like when we're doing *zazen,* our sitting meditation: exhalation, inhalation, exhalation, inhalation, exhalation . . .

Aren't we doing the same thing as the whale?

Last night during *zazen* I couldn't help but hear the crickets, and later I thought about the "cricket man" whom I met on Sonoma Mountain Road a few years ago. He said he was looking for a place to live. He longed to live in some rural area where he could hear the sound of the crickets. I spoke to him only that one time, but our conversation left a deep impression on me because I realized that that's where I'm living. And there are one million, trillion crickets here! But just like the whales that pass by Salt Point, gliding on the rhythm of their breath, the crickets have a natural flow and energy behind their activity, because, in their own way, the crickets are doing something like our practice of *shikan taza,* where we sit wholeheartedly with our entire being. The whales are also doing *shikan taza.* The lotuses in the pond are doing *shikan taza.* And just as with all other things, each of these is conveying this enormous transmission of Dharma.

In an interview that a Benedictine monk had with His Holiness in Scotland, he asked the Dalai Lama, "Do you think your sitting on the mountain will be of any good to these twentieth-century people?" The Dalai Lama answered him right away, "Of course. Definitely it is good." It's good because places of meditation are charged with the feeling and the sound of the cricket, or the breathing of the whale, or just our Zen breathing, and this creates a very powerful life force that affects the life of our environment.

While Shinko and I were watching the water splashing up on the rocks and listening to the ancient sound of the waves coming in and out, in and out, as they have for thousands and thousands of years, we could feel it. And last night sitting in the *zendo* surrounded by the sound of all the crickets, I could feel this transmission of energy as well. As His Holiness implied, we should know that a great contribution can be made in this way.

At night here on Sonoma Mountain there are one million individual crickets, just rubbing their legs together, doing cricket *shikan taza*. These crickets work very hard, and as one cricket's legs get a little bit tired, it stops, but then another cricket comes in at exactly the same moment and makes a big "Chirrrp!" If you listen carefully, you'll hear a whole chorus build up. It's like frost gathering on snow. Of course, we all know how small an individual snowflake is, but as these individual snowflakes gather together and frost begins to spread, it is actually transmission of Dharma, of Truth, and pretty soon you can see one whole mountain. That's exactly what occurs when many people practice together, here at the center or anywhere. And those people who are practicing can really feel it.

Right now as I sit here on this bright summer day, there are stars in the sky. I can't see them because in daylight our eyes can't reach that far, but still they are out there, shining. In fact, we are each a star, shining in the sky in this vast universe. Our eyes can't reach the distance, our mind can't really comprehend, so we don't see it, but when we sit like a mountain, it comes to pass that through the crickets, and the whale, and even through the repetitive sound of machinery, we can begin to feel this vast dimension that seems outside ourselves but actually is found right here within us. And if we can see it, recognize it, and experience it, then we begin to know that we are a part of it and that it is part of us, that this vast dimension is our own most intimate depth. Then, even within this ever-changing moment, we will truly know that it is always here.

3

Half Moon Makes
Full Halo

When you are stable in your sitting, your mind joins your
body and becomes peaceful fairly quickly.

WE ARE VERY fortunate to be able to practice here
on Sonoma Mountain, because this mountain is
a wonderful place to view the moon. Of course,
there are many wonderful views of the moon—full moon, half
moon, quarter moon, one-day moon—but my favorite view is
the half moon, especially when it illuminates a full halo around
itself. I used to think that because only one half or one quarter
of the moon was showing, there would be no full halo. But it
turns out that even a twenty-five or fifty percent moon makes a
one hundred percent halo. Whether it is full or not, the moon
reflects that much light.

We should know that it is the same with us. When we cultivate our understanding and become aware of what we are doing,
and actually *see* what is happening within ourselves and around
us, we have that same kind of full halo. We don't have to wait
until we can sit in full lotus, or until we have been sitting for ten
or twenty years, as if only then *something* will happen. Some of

us sit cross-legged, some half lotus, some full lotus, and some Burmese style or in a chair. These are only different views of the same moon. There are people who think that one form is better than the other, but it's not true. We are truly like the moon: Any amount of light makes a full halo.

It can happen at the very beginning of our upright sitting, our *zazen,* when our posture is so settled that it allows our "body and mind" to become seated within itself. After all, the posture of the body is the posture of the mind and this is why taking a good posture is so important. Seated like this, we can rediscover the natural gravity of stability within our bodies. When you are stable in your sitting, your mind joins your body and becomes peaceful fairly quickly. There's no need to try to force it at all. In fact, you can't. When there is no forcing, that's stability itself, and it's called "being here." Just so, the moon is resting in the sky— shining.

授戒

The Art of Receiving

*It may strike us as funny, but there are very few enlightened
people, simply because we cannot receive. When you receive
something, you have to let go of everything, even yourself,
the one who is receiving.*

AWAKENED TRUTH, or Buddhadharma, points out that
the truth is always near at hand, it's always with you,
whether you realize it or not. It just needs to be awakened. But most of us don't believe this, and that's why we have
the Jukai ceremony. When you receive the precepts during
Jukai, it is a confirmation of the self that reminds you that before
you take something, you already have it. In this way receiving the
precepts helps you to acknowledge your intrinsic Buddha
Nature.

The word *jukai* is very interesting. The Chinese character that
we pronounce *ju* implies the act of receiving. This is such a simple word, but in order for us to receive something, we have to
be both present and empty. It's like this glass that I'm holding. It
must be empty to receive the water. And I have to be empty
inside to be filled by the water as I drink. We should know that
water is exactly the same everywhere it is received—the great

oceans, the rivers and clouds—until it returns to its origin, completing a natural circle.

On the right side of the written character *ju* there are two hands: one above the roof, and one beneath it. This is one of the ways in which the ideogram itself emphasizes receiving: two hands. When you hand something to someone, in order for them to receive it, their hand must be empty. And the person must be open and empty as well. As practitioners it is important for us to look into this because when we receive instruction, there may be times when we become defensive and are unable to truly receive. And yet receiving is a very important aspect of life itself. No one can exist without receiving.

If you look on the left side of the character *ju,* you'll see another character that actually means "hand," so the whole character contains three hands. It's interesting because the diagonal stroke on the left side refers to a pruning action. The first time our *sangha* took care of our vineyard, we were afraid to really cut and prune the vine. I don't have a background in horticulture, and it was difficult to decide which branches to cut. After ten or twelve years, though, we learned from our mistakes. We learned that the more severely we pruned in winter, the greater the growth in spring. This is true for many aspects of our practice, which help us to burn the fuel of delusion. And it is an essential part of receiving. Before you receive, you must cut. Now in the vineyard we knock out the old dead wood and cut all the excessive growth. We cut it, and we feel it as it falls to the ground.

It's just like what we do in our *zazen* practice. We practice the same thing over and over again until the mind becomes very soft and spacious. When this occurs, less thinking is taking place, which allows our body/mind to feel its original nature. Pretty soon all the old projections and tapes that we carry around just begin falling to the ground, all the excessive activity of the mind, falling to the ground. This word, *ju,* is very good. "To cut," "to open," "to empty," and "to receive" are all expressed by *ju.* This active participation invites the light to come into the vine.

The word *receive* is also very good. When I looked it up in the dictionary, it said that *re* means "back" and *ceive* is "take." In terms of receiving Jukai, then, where what we are receiving is our Buddha Nature, our original nature, we take back what belongs to us, which means it has always been there. In this way it has the same meaning as *realize* or *realization.* It may strike us as funny, but there are very few enlightened people, simply because we cannot receive. When you receive something, you have to let go of everything, even yourself, the one who is receiving. Past, present—yes! even the present!—and future, everything must go. Then we have true receiving. Some of us operate from a more idealistic standpoint and think, "When everything is gone from my mind, then *that* is receiving." But often it may not happen that way. This is important to understand. When we are receiving something, and a few thoughts rush in between and rush out again, we receive it with those rushing thoughts as well. They are included because that's what's happening. Receiving includes a very wide range, as wide as the universe itself.

In the Jukai ceremony students receive a halterlike garment called a *rakusu.* Every morning of practice, just before chanting the *rakusu* verse, which we chant before putting them on, we pick up our folded *rakusus* and place them on the crown of our heads. The *rakusu* is the same as our Buddha Nature, and when we raise it we are invoking our original nature. The *rakusu* is also symbolic of Buddha's mind and body, and the square and rectangular pieces on the major part of the *rakusu* represent delusion and enlightenment. When we sew our *rakusus,* in preparation for receiving

Jukai, we sew them together into one garment. In doing so we are acknowledging that delusion and enlightenment coexist. Actually, because of the interdependent nature of all things, there is no enlightenment outside of delusion.

During this brief chant, right at the point where we say the words "Wearing the Tathagata's* teaching," we remove the *rakusu* from the top of our head, hang the straps around our neck, and place the field of squares and rectangles over the heart area. We cultivate this teaching in the meditation hall, but it does not end there. We make an effort to wear this teaching always by taking it back into the world, into the garden, into our cars, into our work space, into our families, into the dirty dishes. That's how we wear the Tathagata's teaching, and it's the only way. Wearing the teaching means that saving all sentient beings is possible; once you are free, everyone else is free as well, because you are the beholder of all these beings. This is made possible by the way you stand, the way you walk, the way you place your palms together and *gassho,* the way you eat, and even by the way you blow your nose. Yes, in this way you will save all beings. Your practice will inspire people. That's the Mahayana principle so central to Buddhism: saving all sentient beings. The word *saving* does not refer to a religious act. Rather, it evokes urgency, because most people are drowning in their delusional ignorance without knowing that their suffering was created by themselves. Of course, it's easier for you to imagine saving someone besides yourself, but as you are saving somebody else without being attached to the *idea* of saving, just by immersing yourself in the action itself, you are included.

His Holiness the Dalai Lama says one reason he offers the

---

*Tathagata is one of the names for Buddha, meaning "thus come" or "thus gone": in a way, a nondual oneness of neither going nor coming.

Kalachakra ceremony, which includes techniques for transforming each participant's body, speech, and mind into complete
altruistic expressions, is that he feels it has some effect on the
environment. We might understand Jukai, and our other practices, the same way. When we do these practices, when we take
Jukai and receive the precepts, we're not consciously trying to
affect the environment, but everything is affected nonetheless.
Our receiving is felt everywhere. This is the never-ending meaning and spirit of our way.

5

RENUNCIATION

Renunciation does not mean turning our back on the world. It means turning our back on the conditions that cause suffering—greed, anger, and ignorance—and rediscovering our natural confidence through seated meditation.

IN DOGEN-ZENJI'S *Shobogenzo* there is a story about Sogyanandai Daiosho, the Seventeenth Ancestor in our Zen lineage. It is said that when Sogyanandai was born, he had the ability to speak almost immediately. As time went by, it was clear to all who knew him that he was not only a very bright child but was also quite gifted. There was some kind of radiance about him that pervaded his presence and was not just charisma. (His Holiness the Dalai Lama has said that charisma is not a spiritual characteristic, so be aware.) Some kind of light was emanating from this child.

When he was seven years old, Sogyanandai went to his mother and father, the king and queen, and told them of his wish to undergo the process of renunciation, or to take *shukke,* as it is known in Japanese. But of course, his parents flatly refused him. Nonetheless renunciation was all this little boy could think of. So his parents negotiated with him, and as a compromise it was decided that a teacher would be brought to the palace to teach him the Dharma.

For the next nineteen years the boy studied with the teacher, but he was still not satisfied. His wish remained strongly within him. One evening Sogyanandai, who was now twenty-six years old, was looking out the window and saw the sun setting. It cast a warm pinkish-golden color that glowed on the dry grass landscape as it does here on Sonoma Mountain. As he was looking out, he saw that this golden glow was shining on a long, flat road nearby. Suddenly he jumped up and left the palace. He walked many miles and came to a cliff where he entered a cave, sat down, and immediately entered great peace—*samadhi*. This is where you go beyond thought and focus on the calm, quiet, and spacious nature of your true mind, which is always there. Sogyanandai sat in this cave of emptiness for ten years before the great teacher Ragorata Daiosho visited him and confirmed his realization.

Those were the conditions of this young boy, who later became our Seventeenth Ancestor, leaving home. He had a very deep way-seeking mind and also the determination and courage to fulfill his innermost request.

While the Chinese ideogram for *shukke* means "leaving home," this word also means "renunciation." It may sound like a heavy word. What does it mean to you? Does it mean "I can't do all the things I wish to do?" Contrary to what we might think, renunciation is not antilife but refers to a *way* of living that gives life. It's like this *zazen* hall, or *zendo,* which is very austere. Because it's so empty, you can fill it with anything. Properly understood, renunciation is the same; it is life-giving and life-supporting instead of life-denying. Through renunciation we can appreciate everything from the smallest grain of rice to the largest of dharmas.

Often when people hear this word, they shudder and think, "I could never leave the world behind." But renunciation does not mean turning our back on the world. It means turning our back on the conditions that cause suffering—greed, anger, and ignorance—and rediscovering our natural confidence through seated meditation. When we feel the confidence and love within ourselves and in other people, there's no need to harm others and no reason to abuse our minds. It's the gentlest and kindest way to live in this difficult world. Because we are kind and appreciative, which are expressions of our inherent basic goodness, we are also able to be aware and to see clearly. This is really the secret of how to live thoroughly. And because we know how to live thoroughly, we know how to mentally die while living and being renewed over and over again. This is the wonder of practice and the wonder of our lives.

In an ancient Chinese text written by Changlu Zongze, the *Zennen Shingi,* which is the daily regulations for conduct in a Zen monastery, it says, "All the buddhas of the past, present, and future have renounced the world and found the true Way." This very brief but profound statement means that realization and renunciation are synonymous. This is true for everyone—all Buddhas and Bodhisattvas—not only for those who are ordained. The relationship between renunciation and realization is very important to understand. Renunciation is the essence of the Dharmas because through renunciation we give up the dualistic conditions and strong ideas of self that separate us from reality. This is exactly what we are surrendering.

Don't you think that's a good idea? Are you satisfied with how your mind is? My mind is not different from yours, but I may understand it in a different way. It feels good to know how to work with the unwanted feelings and thoughts that arise, to know how to be with them and how much time to spend with them. If we're not sufficiently aware, this endless fabrication will take our life. The choice is ours. As it says, "All the buddhas [who are none other than you and me] of the past, present, and future have renounced the world and found the true Way." That's the path of realization.

In the same section of Dogen's *Shobogenzo* as the story of Sogyanandai there is a passage about Mahakashyapa, the first successor of Shakyamuni Buddha. He is the person to whom the Buddha entrusted the lineage and his understanding in what is called mind-to-mind transmission of the "True Dharma Eye." Mahakashyapa was already over one hundred years old, but even at this late age he wanted to join the *sangha* and renounce the world. One day Shakyamuni said to some monks and especially to Mahakashyapa because he was so old and was already very wise, "'Oh, monks, you've come so far.' Suddenly the hair on their heads fell off, and the *okesa* [Buddha's robe] appeared on their bodies." This is an example of how we are brought away or separated from delusion when we are engaged in the Buddhadharma. Something just wakes us up! It may be something like Sogyanandai seeing the warm, golden light glowing on the dusty road, but it can also be just seeing a newly shaven head in the *zendo* or hearing a car pass by in the street just outside your door.

Dogen goes on to say that *Anuttara samyak sambodhi,* which is the phrase found in the Heart Sutra referring to ultimate awareness or supreme enlightenment, is attained the moment you truly renounce the world and receive the precepts. He is really quite definitive about this and says, "There is no other way." So again realization, or *Anuttara samyak sambodhi,* and renunciation of the world are synonymous. Dogen explains that "there is no opposition between our initial awakening of mind, supreme enlightenment, and the act of renouncing the world." No opposition at all. They are one.

He then quotes from the thirteenth chapter of the Mahaprajna Paramitopadesa Sutra. "Once when Buddha was staying at the Garden of Jetavana, an intoxicated Brahman came up to the Buddha and asked to become his disciple. The Buddha instructed the monks to shave his head and give him an *okesa*. The next day the Brahman awakened from his drunken stupor and was shocked to find himself with his head shaved and dressed in strange clothes. He immediately got up and ran away. Soon after, several monks approached the Buddha and asked him, 'Why did you allow that drunken man to receive the precepts? Now he's run away. Who knows what will happen to him?' Shakyamuni replied, 'I knew he had no intention of renouncing the world and receiving the precepts, and that he did so last night only because he was drunk; nevertheless, because he was moved to renounce the world—even for that short time—he will someday become a true monk. You must be aware of how close is the relationship between renunciation of the world and the eventual attainment of *Anuttara samyak sambodhi.*'" Dogen concludes, "Shakyamuni meant that the essence of the teaching is contained in the act of renouncing the world."

At the moment of renunciation, therefore, you have to die and give up. And in a way that is ordination. There's no way around it for anyone. You have to renounce. When I came to Zen, I wasn't interested in renouncing. I was interested in becoming a strong person, hearing great philosophy, and having something to talk about. I didn't come to renounce. But this is what it's about. Dogen really emphasizes the point by writing that when various people devoted themselves to the Dharma, they actually preserved the Dharma, which was contained in their renunciation of the world. And that *then* they received the precepts. It was not just a mental thing, you understand. Dogen says that the teaching of the Buddha actually permeated their bodies and minds. As a result of their devotion and practice, nearly twenty-six hundred years later people like us have also been able to wear *okesa* and receive the precepts. We should know this and appreciate how long this practice of renunciation went on before it was given to us, and how long it will continue after us.

6

BUDDHA'S LIFE-GIVING PRECEPTS

When we maintain the precepts and the spirit of the precepts in how we walk, how we sit, how we eat, how we talk, and how we relate to one another and to our environment, their constant presence brings light to our lives.

SEEN FROM THE OUTSIDE, it may appear that the precepts are just a set of rules that we are expected to follow. "Don't lie. Don't steal. Don't do this. And especially don't do that!" But that's not the spirit of the precepts at all. The precepts are not just a list of ways to behave that someone else reads to you and expects you to follow. If you take a careful look at the very first precept, you will see what I mean.

The first precept is the most important of them all because it includes the others. Of course, in time you will come to see that each of the precepts really includes the others as well, just as one color reflects all the other colors, but the first precept makes this very clear. It says simply, "Don't kill." But don't kill what? In considering this precept, we should not limit its meaning to the killing of people or animals. It really means "Don't kill your Buddha Nature. Don't kill your life-force." Once you see the depth of this precept, then of course you will have a differ-ent relationship to your entire environment; to people, to ani-mals, to thoughts and feelings, and to everything. Then you will know that there's nothing to steal and that there are no lies to be told. But again it's not something that comes to you from the outside. It comes from that intrinsic part of yourself that longs to live in a full, deep, and meaningful way.

The precepts are like an ignition, and your life is like a can-dle or a lamp without fire. Once it is ignited, you have light. Most of us have many abilities, many ways to seek satisfaction in our lives. We know how to drive a car. We know how to go down the mountain and shop at the mall. More and more of us can use a computer. We take care of our kids. But what do we need to really be satisfied in a very deep way? In the *Shobogenzo* Dogen pointed toward the answer when he wrote that all of the ances-tors kept the precepts. They kept them and manifested them throughout every aspect of their lives; in their thoughts, their actions, their attitudes. It is the same for us. When we maintain the precepts and the spirit of the precepts in how we walk, how we sit, how we eat, how we talk, and how we relate to one another and to our environment, their constant presence brings light to our lives. Living in this way not only keeps the precepts alive, it keeps us alive, as well as all those near and, seemingly, far away.

Let me give you an example of how the precepts may work in your life. Some people like to eat meat, while others never touch it. But actually both eating meat and not eating meat are violations of the precepts. Isn't that just beautiful? This is truly the middle way because it goes beyond dualistic things like good and evil, or attraction and repulsion, et cetera, which causes us suffering. Rather than insisting that we have *our* way, the precepts transform us and bring us real freedom. Therefore, far from being a list of rules that restrict or deaden our lives, the true precepts are life-giving, each one expressing our true nature, and that's their real meaning (see appendix).

7

YOUR TEACHER IS FOUND
IN YOUR PRACTICE

When a student is a student of Zen, their practice should
help them to forget that they are a Zen student. This is
like forgetting the self. When you forget the self, you
become a free and ordinary person.

A s ZEN HAS developed in the West, there have been many discussions on the subject of the relationship between teachers and students. Since the nature of the intimate bond between these two is so important in study and practice alike, it is crucial that these discussions continue so that relationships that are appropriate and right can be established. Just before a teacher gives a Dharma talk, the community of practitioners, known as the *sangha,* chant, "The Dharma, incomparably profound and infinitely subtle, is rarely met, even in a hundred, thousand, million *kalpas.*" A *kalpa* is an immeasurable period of time, sometimes compared to an aeon.

When we say these words, we are really evoking the almost unimaginable boundlessness of the Dharma, and yet such boundlessness means nothing other than yourself. One of your teacher's most important jobs, if not the most important one, is to point you in the direction of yourself so you can see for yourself. In order for this to be possible, a special kind of intimate bond must be established between you as a student and the teacher. Your teacher must truly know your heart and mind. And likewise you should know the teacher's heart and mind; that means, of course, that you know your own heart and mind as well, which is the same heart and mind of all things.

In order to help us to understand more about the student-teacher relationship, Suzuki-roshi used to tell us one of his favorite stories about Isan-zenji, who comes from the lineage of Hui Neng (Taikan Eno in Japanese), the Sixth Ancestor. Isan was resting one hot summer afternoon, just kind of dozing in his room, when his disciple Kyozan walked by and peeked inside. When he saw him, Isan said, "Oh, Kyozan, don't think that you'll bother me, please come in." Kyozan came in, and when he was settled, Isan said, "I had a wonderful dream. Do you want to know what my dream was?" Without saying anything, Kyozan stood up and went out to get a pan of water and a face cloth. Then he came back into Isan's room and offered it to his teacher. His teacher dipped the cloth in the cool water, wiped his face, and felt joyously refreshed.

Just about this time Isan's other disciple, Kyogen, walked by, looked in, and saw the two of them. "Can I come in?" he asked. "Oh, yes," Isan said, "please join us." When Kyogen was settled, he proceeded to ask the same question of him: "I just had a wonderful dream," Isan told him. "Do you want to know what it was?" Immediately Kyogen went into the next room, made some tea, and brought it in. Then the three of them all drank tea together.

That's the story. But also this is the exact life of Zen.

It's very different from when we ask someone about their

dream, or when our friend asks if we had a dream, and what kind of dream it was. If we are not familiar with Dharma, we may tell a long story about our great dream, including all the details we can remember, and then begin to interpret and speculate about what it could possibly mean. Isn't that so? But each student—or in the case of this story, each disciple—awakens the present moment. This present moment is the dream. Our lives are not about another dream. If it is a hot day, we could use a cloth dipped in cool water, or on a hot day perhaps you might boil someone a pot of hot tea. That is the meaning of relationship, and it's a very good illustration of a deep student-teacher relationship.

This story also means that the student is independent. The students weren't interested in the dream of their teacher. In fact, they didn't even think about it; what they did in the situation was a simple and natural response. When a student is a student of Zen, their practice should help them to forget that they are a Zen student. This is like forgetting the self. When you forget the self, you become a free and ordinary person. And so on a hot summer day you can bring someone a cool face cloth and serve some hot tea.

It is important when you study that you have faith in the teacher, because the teacher is the connection to the Buddhadharma. But usually people have some natural difficulty in this area. They are afraid of the teacher, or they have some large projection onto the teacher that keeps them from seeing who the teacher really is, which makes the teacher appear larger than life. Zen teachers aren't really concerned with having people worship them or treat them as deities or as sacred beings. But since we are all students, we should know that when we do regard someone or something as sacred or holy, we are also acknowledging that aspect within ourselves. Since we can see the sacredness in others, we uphold this conviction within ourselves. And that is what happens when we bow before an altar or shrine, or when we bow to each other. We must remember this fact, otherwise we lose our real relationship to people and to things and the meaning of what real practice is all about.

When students practice in a *sangha,* it is very important that they relate directly to the teacher. But students must also relate to the Dharma, the teaching on the path, and to the *sangha* of practitioners. Every teacher will tell you that there are many different kinds of students. Some students don't relate to the teacher, or to the Buddha aspect of the practice, but they do relate to the Dharma teaching and to the *sangha* as part of their circle of friends. Some relate just to the *sangha*; they don't connect with the Buddha or the Dharma. As a real student, however, it's important that you relate to all three equally. It's like a rainbow; when you see a rainbow, you see many different colors, but you don't favor one. The colors appear in the transparent form of a bow, and they can't really be separated. That's why a rainbow is so wondrous and beautiful. This is a very important point, one that I encourage you to work on. In time, through your experience, I trust you will see the value of the Three Treasures: Buddha, Dharma, and Sangha. In this way they become your own.

My relationship with Suzuki-roshi lasted for only eleven years. Eleven years is a very brief period of time to know someone in a truly intimate way, and when I studied with Suzuki-roshi, I imagine it was similar to the way many people practice. I had a family, and I worked in the world, and I saw him every day except Sundays. But really I had no idea what I was actually studying; at least, that's what I thought. I knew that something drew me to the Zen Center, and certainly part of it was my love for Suzuki-roshi, but it was more of a personal thing. I didn't really see or appreciate the *sangha*; nor did I see the Dharma very well. I think I saw the Dharma somewhat, and it was immaculate, it was a great treasure, but I wasn't able to apply this immaculate teaching and practice to my life. Honestly, what good is all of this, the Three Treasures, if with the background of constant practice you cannot at some time make them work within your life?

In 1960, when we had our very first formal week-long periods of practice known as *sesshin* (this word literally means "to touch the heart/mind"), I realized that I could put 108 percent of myself into the retreat, but when I came home, I could hardly lift my finger. I felt very discouraged. Still, from this experience, which I know is a common one, we must develop a sense of constancy. The journey is very long. It's not a short trip where we bring our lunch boxes. We have to think of it as a more-than-ten-lifetimes journey; even when you think your lifetime is finished, it's not finished.

With my projection onto the teacher and not really seeing or appreciating the Three Treasures, I have to admit that I was not aware of what I was doing. But intuitively that may be why I kept going to the Zen Center. I hardly missed one day in eleven years, sitting every morning. When I met Suzuki-roshi, it was the first time I encountered someone's complete presence, someone I felt I could trust completely. Because I trusted this person, I could also give to this person. What was best about this giving is that the gift was not just what *I* liked, but also what *he* liked. So there was a meeting between us.

We can learn a lot from this kind of practice. Once you give a gift and it has left your hand, it belongs to the other person, and he or she does what they want with it, because it's theirs. One time I gave Suzuki-roshi a very old and beautiful Korean celadon vase. He thanked me for it that day, but afterward I never saw it again. "Gee, where is it?" I wondered. It turned out that he had given it to somebody else! Now it really makes me laugh. But that's giving: Once it leaves your hands, it's gone. The act is done, and you should be happy.

There are a few more things I'd like to mention in connection with the student-teacher relationship. First, faith is one of the four legs of practice. Faith is not an idea, it is something that is proven over and over again through your physical practice until it seeps into your body. Dogen called it our "faithlike body," which is exactly right.

In the Buddhadharma there are three parts to faith. Faith in your teacher is an essential part because the teacher connects you to the Buddhadharma. The second part is faith in yourself. Again, the faith within recognizes the faith without; how could you be aware of it if it weren't within you? You must begin to have confidence in yourself, not just in who you think you are but in who you may be. I hear people say all kinds of things about themselves—"I can't remember" or "My mind is not very good" or "I can't do this"—but actually your Buddha Nature is everything. So I remind you that you have learned this way of thinking about yourself, and it is a mistake; you must remember that you *can* do. After all Buddha, your own awakening, is the one who does it, not "you." Therefore you can let this deceptive thinking go. This faith is rooted in the teaching that, even despite our dualistic thinking, what we are really is so.

You must have faith in yourself, and you must practice so that it will grow. It is very important, because when you have this faith in yourself, you can study the self and realize the self. Even faith in the small self in its narrow sense is good; faith that this "I," this small "I," can do something. Hopefully your relationship with your teacher will encourage you to take this leap of faith in yourself right where you are.

The third part is to have faith in the method, faith in *zazen*. Suzuki-roshi spoke a lot about *zazen* practice, and he didn't just mean sitting cross-legged. He meant to take what you know of the practice into your life and not to forget it. You must apply it to all parts of your life. Dogen-zenji said that physical sickness does not destroy a person, but when you do not practice, or you do not sit, or you do not apply the awareness to your everyday activity, then you will end up destroying your life.

There is a story about a man named Seiko who loved dragons. He built his house in the shape of a dragon. He made paper dragon kites and told dragon stories to children. He also loved to carve dragons. His reputation grew far and wide. One day, sure enough, a dragon flew by and saw the shape of his house and said, "Oh, I should visit this man, because he'll be very pleased to see me." So the dragon descended and knocked on his door, and when Seiko opened the door and saw the dragon, he cried, *"Ohhhhhhhh!"* And this scared the dragon away.

This story is about how we love the paper dragons, or our fantasies, our endless and infinite fantasies. We love them and are attached to them. We love to entertain them, but we don't want to face the true dragon when it appears before us. Let me assure you that once our practice and training have matured, we can distinguish between what looks real and what is real. We sit every day, but what are we *really* doing is the point. What are we doing? You can sit a whole lifetime without coming close to yourself. You can spend a whole lifetime entertaining a paper dragon, but it's only a picture of your Self. We must truly face ourselves in *zazen*. And we must learn to renew our sitting, over and over and over again. Do not think that once you feel you've gotten someplace in your practice, you can say, "Oh, this is the place," and assume that you know what sitting is, or that you've got it down, because things are always changing. This is a very serious matter; in fact, it is the great matter, specifically if you study Zen.

Please endeavor to find your teacher in every part of your practice. As it says in one of our chants, "Buddha Nature pervades the whole universe," so you can be certain that your teacher is really there. Even if your teacher has died, it doesn't mean that the teacher is gone, because the heart and mind of a teacher are forever the heart and mind of Zen.

8

SPIRIT OF COOKING

There's a spirit that we shouldn't lose, and whether we're just making things up as we go along or someone is right there showing us the way, that spirit holds something important for us in our everyday life.

ONE DAY IN 1960 when I was the cook, or *tenzo,* before we officially became the San Francisco Zen Center, Suzuki-roshi came into the kitchen to show me how to cook rice gruel. This is a common dish that is usually eaten by southern Chinese people. After the rice is cooked, a crust is left on the bottom of the pot. Once the rice is eaten, this crust is toasted so that, with the addition of hot water, it can also be eaten after dinner. Some people like it so much, they eat it as a meal in itself.

I may have been about twenty-five years old at the time, and so as Suzuki-roshi was teaching me how to cook the gruel, I said, "Yes, I know how to do that!" Of course, I didn't say it quite that way, but he could tell by my manner that this was what I meant. Even so he persisted in demonstrating to me in detail, step by step, as we stood side by side in Mrs. Suzuki's kitchen. He wasn't just showing me how to cook the rice, of course; he was demonstrating a kind of teacher-student relationship to me, and through it he was telling me, "Follow my mind. This is how it is." I have to admit that at the time it felt like being squeezed, though I know he did it out of his wisdom and compassion. This lesson stays with me still to this day.

In general Suzuki-roshi did not tell me what to do in the kitchen. He explained only one or two rituals, because the *tenzo* also has that responsibility. For example, during *sesshin* he said to come out of the kitchen with the *kaishaku,* the ritual wooden sticks used to indicate the start of the formal *oryoki*** meal, strike them together three times, bow, and then serve the food. He made it very clear that this had to be done on time. The rest of the ritual demanded only that we be attentive and aware, taking care of the various needs that arose during the entire meal. As with other parts of our practice, the quality of our awareness and attention determined how we went about our various tasks. Looking back on it, I have to say we attempted to do things not in the most efficient way but in the way that was most harmonious and reverent.

We reflected on which way to point the spout of the teapot, how to line up the pots before serving tea, and which utensils to use with rice and which with salad. We were also attentive to how we placed the utensils on the table. Suzuki-roshi usually remained silent. He left me alone and seemed to have confidence in what I was trying to do. This is one way of teaching, and actually not saying very much to a student can be a good way. As a result of this training, however, I have to admit that sometimes I forget that it's also good to show someone how to do something,

---

Oryoki literally means "just the right amount" or "just enough" and refers to a monk's set of bowls used during the eating of a ritual meal.

or to do it alongside of them. They cut onions; you cut onions with them. That's how we learn from each other.

We were sitting in the old Soko-ji temple, and our *sesshins* were attended by up to 125 people. After all the spots for sitting in the temple filled up, students sat all the way down the balcony and flowed downstairs into the theater. We had two family-size refrigerators—one was about three hundred feet away, down a narrow flight of stairs near the back of the temple—and we had only one five-burner stove. Formal *oryoki* sets that include the three bowls, special cloths, and utensils hadn't been introduced yet, so we ate on baby-blue plastic GI trays, one tray for each person, with regular dishes and utensils alongside a Buddha bowl. There was no special utensil, called the *setsu,* for cleaning our bowls at the end of the meal, so we cleaned with a pickled vegetable held by our chopsticks. In the kitchen we had done our best to provide a meal where the size and shape of the food, the color and texture, would add to its nourishment. Then each person was served rice, miso soup with tofu, pickles, sautéed vegetables, and whatever else we could put together, all for the sake of the spirit of practice.

That may not sound like very professional Zen, but it was good because I learned that if you think about something too much, it becomes bewildering, but when you "just do it," it's not so bad. Maybe we should go back to the baby-blue trays and to improvising as we go along. That's a joke, of course, but there's a spirit that we shouldn't lose, and whether we're just making things up as we go along or someone is right there showing us the way, that spirit holds something important for us in our everyday life.

9

Breaking the Skin Born of Mother

If they come as the light, I become one with the light.
If they come as the dark, I become one with the dark.
Before you can think!

OST PEOPLE HAVE two kinds of practice. One may be called personal practice, and the other is Dharma practice. Dharma practice is one of the most important things for us to cultivate because it is the essence of our lives. When we come together as a *sangha,* we must not forget that the direction we have chosen, our purpose, is the Bodhisattva path. Your intention to help others is the main cause of your own salvation. People suffer because they are always thinking of themselves and remain caught in their own problems. Dharma practice means forgetting your problems through helping others. It also means that your personal practice becomes transformed into real practice. Dharma practice is not just something you read about; it's something that we actualize in daily life. When we do actualize it, we begin to recognize the stability that was always there. No matter what is going on, we feel stable and calm. That comes from Dharma practice. Again, it's not something we think about, or even try to accomplish, but as we practice *zazen,* specifically *zazen,* we will experience it. This is the kernel or the heart of Dharma practice.

By emphasizing Dharma practice, I don't mean to imply that members of a *sangha* can't be friends with each other. Of course we should become friends. But once you root in Dharma practice, or clear direction, it becomes your common denominator, the basis for everything in your life. We should find out what our denominator is and remember what kind we have.

In high school my good friend Ed Jones and I would go out in his 1940 blue Ford convertible, park under the stars, reflect on the universe, and discuss philosophy. We would try to think of the thing most common to all things and nonthings. At that time we came to the conclusion that it was space. Although it was just an idea, for people so young it wasn't too bad. But to have some kind of common denominator, or Dharma practice, is to directly experience the commonality of all things within yourself.

At the Zen Center we have a community where people are nice and kind. We make humorous jokes, and we care for each other in a wonderful way. We provide food and shelter as well as interesting things to think about, but the most crucial thing that we are able to develop and cultivate as a *sangha* is Dharma practice.

There are two stories, very old ones, I'd like to tell you. These stories are invaluable to us because they help to inspire us, through practice, to really find out what sitting upright is all about. In your life you will meet all kinds of teachers, and you'll meet all kinds of friends, and your path will cross other paths, but the most important thing is the common denominator that helps you to know what is genuine. When you train well, you can discern the difference between what looks real and what is real. It's simple but also very difficult to discern what looks real from what actually is real. From your training and practice, this quality, which is nothing other than your own awareness, will emerge.

One part of the practice that leads to this understanding is not avoiding difficulty. Again, when I was in high school, if I was walking down the hallway and saw somebody coming whom I didn't like, I would make an extra effort to go down another hallway to avoid confronting that person. But sooner or later that person would always show up somewhere else. In our lives whatever difficulty we are trying to avoid seems like it always returns. Isn't it true? But through your own training and practice, you're able to face these difficulties. By facing them, based on the common denominator of the Dharma, you will rediscover your basic goodness and form good character. But it's *only* through encountering difficulty that this happens.

A good example of Dharma practice and difficulty was reflected in an open letter that the former head of the San Francisco Dharmadhatu Community, Alan Schwartz, wrote to their *sangha* after their teacher, Chögyam Trungpa Rinpoche, died. Schwartz said, "A perspective that often seems to be forgotten these days is that it has ALWAYS been somewhat touchy or painful to approach a Dharma situation. Even when we saw Rinpoche's most charming smile, those teeth loomed large. Approaching him wasn't entertaining—it was often frightening or intimidating. That fear was our own resistance to being simple, being naked, being genuine. When we are willing to face our own discomfort as the simple, unglamorous truth of our experience, though we twist and turn and struggle, our practice is to stick with it until we give in and let go. When we do, our minds open outward, the Dharma is born, and blessings descend. In Shambhala terms, this is the discovery of warriorship."

This first story is about what is real and what looks real. It is essentially a dialogue that took place between Dogen's teacher Tendo Nyojo and Tendo Nyojo's teacher Seccho Chikan. It is also the source of Dogen's famous saying *Shinjin datsuraku, datsuraku shinjin,* or "Body-mind drop off, mind-body drop off."

Dogen's enlightenment took place when he was sitting at Tendo Nyojo's temple in China. The meditation hall there is a good size, with a stone-cut floor and an altar in the center. Tendo Nyojo, the abbot at the temple, sat facing outward directly behind the altar. Many evenings Tendo Nyojo had the disciples practice *zazen* late into the night. When we practice meditation together as a *sangha,* we greatly affect one another, and I don't just mean that a little bit of silence spreads through the *zendo,* because at times it seems like that silence is all pervasive. As we sit together, the meditation hall becomes more and more quiet, and although it is already calm, somehow the feeling of silence and calm deepens. In actuality, this feeling of pervasiveness is us.

On one particular night of late practice the monk next to Dogen was falling asleep. Tendo Nyojo noticed this, so he stood up, walked over to the monk with his slipper, struck him on the shoulder, and said, "*Zazen* is not sleeping! *Zazen* is mind and body drop off. Body and mind drop off." *Shinjin datsuraku, datsuraku shinjin.* As soon as his teacher said that, Dogen awakened.

One day Seccho Chikan and his student, Tendo Nyojo, were having a Dharma dialogue. Even when it's not formal, students and teachers are always having a Dharma dialogue, because that's an important part of practice. Seccho Chikan asked, "It is originally unsoiled, so how can it be cleaned?" In other words, your Buddha Nature, your inherent nature, or basic goodness, is immaculately pure, so how can you clean it? Then he went on to tell Tendo Nyojo, "If you climb out of your rut, you will be free. The former enlightened masters originally didn't bring about partial understanding. Committed to the single truth, they got people to practice with one objective, without self-concern. If for the entire twenty-four hours of the day, there is no view of purity or defilement, you are naturally undefiled." Seccho Chikan was encouraging his student to understand that if for one whole day and night you think neither good nor bad, you are already your true self through and through. "However, Tendo Nyojo still had not escaped the view of defilement. He held on to the idea of using a broom to sweep it away. After a year of keeping this koan within himself, when there was no more skin to shed, nor mind and body that needed to be shed, he said to Seccho Chikan, 'I hit upon that which is unsoiled.'" And his teacher hit him before he finished his sentence. After all, who is it that is originally unsoiled? And what does this actually mean?

This is a wonderful dialogue because mirroring each other is one of the most intimate things we have to offer. If you're sad, I feel sad. If you're happy, I feel very happy. If you're clear, I feel clear. If you're dull, I feel dull. This is the process of seeing *things as it is,* which is a phrase Suzuki-roshi often used. Because we're able to see *things as it is,* we are not attached to them. Things do come and go. Usually people grasp what they see and hold on to it. Through true practice we become less opinionated and less judgmental. Even though we have opinions, they're not so self-centered, and we see with the eye of compassion.

It was an enlightened mind that caused Seccho Chikan to hit Tendo Nyojo even before he finished speaking. As soon as he was struck, "Tendo Nyojo felt the sweat break out all over his body. He lost his body at once. His body felt like it disappeared, and he found the power. Truly he realized that he was intrinsically pure, and had never been subject to impurity. This is why he always said that the practice of Zen is dropping off body and mind."

You will meet many people and encounter many different teachers who have been trained in different ways. As a result you may become more skillful and sophisticated. But *this* kind of experience is very simple, direct, and authentic. Sweat broke out over the entire body. This is beyond our dualistic thinking. This is real.

I remember one day in the late 1960s when I was at Tassajara, the Zen Mountain Center near Big Sur, California, founded by Suzuki-roshi, I saw two students, a monk and a lay person, walking down the path. The monk was wearing his robes and *okesa,* which is Buddha's robe draped over the left shoulder, and the lay student was walking with his arm over the monk's *okesa.* At the time I didn't see anything wrong with that. I thought, "How wonderful. What a good, warm relationship." But there's another kind of relationship that we should understand. It's just like when we eat *oryoki.* When we eat with the Buddha bowl, which is symbolic of Buddha's head, we don't eat from it by putting our lips to it. In fact, the edge of the bowl curves slightly inward so that we can't. This has to do with a deeper relationship, a relationship we might think of as "without touching." Usually when we like something, we create a subject and object. We touch to become one. But in Zen there's another way that can be called "without touching." It means we already are one. Do you understand?

This next reading comes from *The Lancet of Seated Meditation, Zazen-shin,* written by Wanshi Shogaku, the great eleventh-century Chinese Zen master who introduced "silent illumination," the practice of the Soto Zen school. This excerpt, taken from *Dogen's Manual of Zen Meditation* by Carl Bielefeldt, will offer you some understanding on "without touching":

It knows without touching things. Knowing, here, of course does not mean perception. For perception is of little measure. It does not mean understanding, for understanding is artificially constructed. Therefore, this knowing is not touching things. And not touching things is real knowing. Such knowing should not be measured as even universal knowledge. It should not be categorized as self-knowledge. This not touching means when they come in the light, I hit them in the light; when they come in the dark, I hit them in the dark. It means sitting and breaking the skin born of mother.

In the way of Zen we say "hit-sit." This is the *ta-za* in *shikan taza,* or wholehearted sitting with our entire being. *Ta* means "to hit" or "to meet," "to become one." *Ta!* And *za* is the same word as in *za-zen,* so it refers to the essence of our seated meditation. *Ta-za!* Hit-sit. We must know what hit-sit means. If I strike my stick on the floor, you will know it: *Bam!* Hit-sit means the same as "Hit them in the light." Another way to say this is: If they come as the light, I become one with the light. If they come as the dark, I become one with the dark. Before you can think! Just like my stick striking the floor: *Bam!* Before you can think!

This story actually comes from Fuke, a close disciple of Rinzai, the ninth-century Chinese Zen master who founded the Rinzai school. In the old days Fuke walked through the streets chanting and shaking his hand bell, and people looked at him as if he were a crazy beggar. But some knew that he wasn't just a beggar; there was something different about him. One of the phrases Fuke would chant was part of what we've just heard in the story: "When they come in the light, I hit them in the light; when they come in the dark, I hit them in the dark."

The sentence "It means sitting and breaking the skin born of mother" may sound most extraordinary. It tells us that through our *zazen* we come to realize we are not just this object, this child who came from our mother. To break the skin born of mother is to break your karma, your bondage, your delusion. It means you break through this person born of your mother. Sometimes it is called being *unborn*. This is real knowing.

There is a Vietnamese Zen master whose name is Thich Man Giac. I believe he may be the patriarch of the North American Vietnamese *sangha*. He could be someone like your good uncle, a very warm, smiling, yet deep person. In 1986, during a ceremony at Rocky Mountain Dharma Center, each of us was handed some flowers. If our mother was alive, we were told, we were to wear the red flower on our lapel, and if our mother had died, we were to wear the white flower. I noticed that Thich Man Giac picked the red flower. Since he was already old, I thought, "Gee, his mother must be really ancient!" Later on I couldn't help but ask him, and he said, "My real mother is Kannon Bosatsu." That's breaking the skin of your mother.

The name Kannon means "the perceiver of all the world's sounds." Kannon Bosatsu's vow, which is so central to our practice, was to postpone her realization until all sentient beings were saved from fear and suffering. So she is the *bosatsu* or Bodhisattva (enlightened being) of mercy and compassion and the mother of all Buddhas.

When you have faith in this kind of mother, your denominator is solid. You're like a real stone through and through that can't be moved. You're in the right relationship, the Dharma relationship, with all things, and this alone makes for a very wondrous and wonderful life.

10

Two Schools, One *Samadhi*

You sit on your black cushion, your mind and body rhythms become slower and slower, quieter and quieter, and you begin to be aware of the one great thing. Everything is simple and direct, and there appears to be much more space from which to live. This is the life of the Great Bodhisattva.

ANY YEARS AGO Suzuki-roshi gave a talk in which he told a story about Zen master Tenryu, who was famous for his "one finger Zen." Each time someone came to ask him a question, Tenryu just held up one finger. That was it. Suzuki-roshi liked to tell us another story as well: It seems that for some time a certain ancient Chinese Zen master didn't give any Dharma talks, or *teisho,* at his monastery. The monks pleaded with him to give a Dharma talk, and finally one day he agreed. When it was time for the *teisho,* he walked into the Dharma hall, offered incense and prostrations in front of the altar, and sat down in his seat. After a few minutes he slowly got up, bowed, and walked out. The disciples there were all rather perplexed, and later on they asked him, "Why didn't you say anything?"

He responded, "I'm not a Dharma teacher; I'm a Zen master."

Stories like these may seem a little mystifying, but they're very instructive for us. That is one of the reasons the Zen tradition has cherished them for so many generations. A tremendous amount of profundity is conveyed by even the simplest of gestures or forms.

The two major traditions or schools of Zen are the Soto and the Rinzai. At Sonoma Mountain Zen Center our practice is rooted in the Soto tradition, which has been called the school of gradual enlightenment. When we speak of our Soto practice, we sometimes call ourselves the school of "silent illumination." For us, the most important thing is how we sit. The practice used in the Rinzai school, the school of sudden enlightenment, is a bit different from ours, or maybe I should say it has a different emphasis, called *huatou* in Chinese: "speech and head" or "head and speech." The method they practice in *zazen* is also called *huatou* or, in Japanese, *koan*. Many people use the word *koan* nowadays to mean some kind of incomprehensible riddle, but what it really means is an "unuttered word" or "that which is before speech." What is significant for us as human beings is to know what actually *is,* what is "before speech," the actual place from which the words and all things arise, and to which they return as well.

Another phrase found in the Rinzai school is "Great Doubt." Rinzai has often been called the school of "Great Doubt." This could mean that, without being attached to it, practitioners in the Rinzai school keep the question *What is it?* alive. This question is similar to what I mentioned just above: What is before anything and everything?

At one time when I was considering the "silent illumination" of the Soto tradition, I thought we could just say "silent" instead of "silent illumination," but true silence is illumination, so we add the word "illumination" to bring this out. When you are sitting, you go through many different phases. When you think you are doing well in your sitting practice, you love your practice; when you are not doing so well in your *zazen,* you hate it, and sometimes you just feel like a robot going through the motions. It is difficult to just sit down and continue to practice. But after a very long while, supported by your vow to not give up, sitting will become one of the most intimate parts of your life. The river really does long to return to the ocean, and so just like Bodhidharma we face the wall and allow the light to turn inward toward our mind source. And at the same time from that vast space of emptiness that is simultaneously *now* and *before anything and everything,* we silently illuminate. As you can see, both schools, Soto and Rinzai, come from the same root.

When you consider Tenryu holding up one finger, it's important that you understand that it was not just the finger he was holding up. This finger includes everything. It is the wondrous finger of the whole universe. That was his great teaching, and that's why he could not exhaust this finger for his entire life. When we sit, it's the same thing; it's not just the sitting that's taking place or being expressed, it's something beyond our selves and our personal limitations. It is not *you* that sits. It is the Buddha sitting *in you* that pervades the whole universe.

In the Soto tradition another word we hear often is *shikan taza.* As I've mentioned, it means "sitting wholeheartedly with our entire being." But this wholehearted sitting, or being, doesn't just happen on the cushion. *Shikan taza* is everywhere. Tenryu holding up one finger and the Zen master who bowed, offered, sat, and walked out of the meditation hall without saying a word were both expressing *shikan taza.*

Samadhi, when you focus on the calm and quiet nature of your mind source, is another word used in our tradition. After you have practiced sitting meditation for a while, you must refine your sitting with *samadhi.* Then when you sit down, you find yourself just sitting in the midst of this quiet and calm. To do so you must let go of all your concerns. Of course, this takes cultivation, and it doesn't happen very often at the beginning of a person's practice, but it is how to really practice *zazen.*

Often when I meet with students during their *dokusan* interview, they say, "I'm fed up with my thinking mind," but little do they know! They do not know that when you're really fed up, you just put it down. You already do this every day each time you turn your attention to something else, one thing after another. The Korean Zen master Seung Sahn used to say, "Put it down!" Over and over again, "Put it down!" We don't put it down, but even when we gather together on Sonoma Mountain waiting for work practice to begin, whether we are standing outside or sitting at the table in chairs, we should use this time to practice putting everything down; thinking about the work, the time of day, our tiredness, our hunger, our plans, everything. Actually, that's *shikan taza.* That's silent illumination, which is really just sitting in a chair.

I've been discussing all these different terms because it's the usual way people describe the Rinzai school and the Soto school, the two legs of Zen. But these are just ways of looking at these two schools. What I really want you to know is that these schools are two expressions of one great thing. So whether someone else practices *huatou* or koan or we practice *shikan taza* or silent illumination, we are basically practicing the same thing. As I said, it all comes from the same root. When the focus of your practice becomes like the light of the sun penetrating a magnifying glass so sharply that it makes a fire, it dissolves greed, anger, and ignorance, the three great obstacles to our original heart/mind. Since these obstacles are no longer there, you become aware of the nature of your original heart/mind, which is vast like an ocean and pervasively very quiet, calm, and bright. Then your attitude and demeanor naturally transform. Surprisingly, more than you had ever known, you realize that you are a kind, gentle, and compassionate person. This true realization, or revelation, is due to *zazen*.

Zen master Rinzai always said, "At this very moment reveal the truth." He also told people, "Don't think you're going to become a Buddha." The worst scenario is when you think that you're going to become enlightened. That's why Rinzai told people, "You are Buddha at this very moment. If at any moment you pass beyond confusion and reveal truth, then you are Buddha."

For us the method by which we "reveal truth" is *zazen* itself. The deeper your *zazen* becomes, the more you will be able to turn on your *samadhi* at will. Even before you sit down with this intention, *it's on*. In addition to the direct focus of *samadhi*, you may also have a softer focus during *zazen* practice, which you are able to do because you've practiced deeply while also cultivating how to put or lay down all concerns. You may be sitting cross-legged or in a chair. You may be standing in a train, sitting on a beach chair, or even walking. It's not dependent on any particular condition.

We say that those in the Rinzai school, the school of Great Doubt, perfect the head, or the top of the body, while we in the Soto school perfect the bottom half, through the legs and stability. Actually, we must do both. We must have the legs for stability and also have the head to turn our light inward, so there is equanimity between the bottom and the top. It expresses one whole.

In our way you cultivate a great sense of confidence and faith through long years of experience in your own physical practice. You don't give up, you keep going straight, because through your practice you will inevitably confront yourself. This is how you refine your life, and at some point, by practicing in this way, you may realize that you've gone beyond even the most fearful place in your mind: fear of a nonexistent self.

Shikan taza is one of the dynamic aspects of Zen sitting. It is like having an objectless goal; there is nothing to gain, no concentration, no self. We just sit in what's been called "objectless awareness" while listening to the sound of our breathing and occasionally reflecting what appears. A number of years ago, from many years of practice, I came up with the saying "Breath sweeps mind." After the breath sweeps the mind, you rediscover the spaciousness that is quiet, calm, and bright and that has always been with you. As Dogen said, "To study the self is to forget the self." But you should not think that sitting practice is being forgetful. Rather, it is laying the self aside like a mother with her newborn. *Samadhi* is the focus of going behind the thought of self into great calm and spaciousness.

Don't you feel greatly relieved to know that you don't have to think about anything and yet you are vividly alive even without thinking? (One thought arising once in a while is no problem.) You sit on your black cushion, your mind and body rhythms become slower and slower, quieter and quieter, and you begin to be aware of the one great thing. Everything is simple and direct, and there appears to be much more space from which to live. This is the life of the Great Bodhisattva.

THE SOUND OF THE BELL

"Each thing has its own intrinsic value." It is with this very same spirit of realization that we approach our work and life.

DURING THE MORE INTENSIVE practice periods one of the things you will feel in the *sangha* is a kind of intimate bonding and communication. This communication is not based on our sitting around telling one another about our lives. It takes place almost entirely without speaking, without touching, even without looking at or seeing one another. It is based on the kind of attention and awareness we bring to our activities. When awareness mirrors our quiet and calm, the communication expressed through the activity is strong and ever present. We become the activity. This kind of presence emerges from our Buddha Nature, and the intimacy and communication can be felt everywhere: the mountains, the animals, the insects, the vegetables in the garden, the trees, and even the clouds. Everything is included in this intimacy and communication and, of course, most important, ourselves.

Morita-zenji was the abbot of Eihei-ji, which was Dogen's thirteenth-century temple and is also the mother temple of all Soto temples. *Zenji* means "Zen teacher" and is an honorific title given to venerable Zen masters when they become abbots of Eihei-ji. When Morita was about twelve or thirteen years old, his father was extremely ill and wanted to provide for his son. His father must have been a very good teacher because he encouraged his son to continue the path, to maintain his resolve, and to go to practice at Eihei-ji. "When you arrive at Eihei-ji," he told his young son, "there are three things they will ask you to do. One thing will be to collect the garbage. The second will be to gather vegetables. The third will be to strike the *bonsho,* the big bell." At Eihei-ji the bell is very big, about the size of a large room, with a deep, sonorous, and mellow sound that resonates so well, it is known for a very long distance.

In a Zen temple or monastery collecting garbage is one of the most important jobs. When we pick up papers or garbage, we have to understand that we are also picking up the garbage inside our own minds. The words *outside* and *inside* are two ways of describing one thing. Since our thoughts and dualistic understanding are a kind of littering in our mind, when we pick one up, we pick both up in exactly the same way. Do you understand? That's our *samu,* which means "work practice," and that's our work. When we pick up the garbage, we pick it up one hundred percent. It's like when lightning strikes the sky—nothing remains. This kind of action affects other people. If we pick it up in a distracted way, with our minds on something else, we just make more litter. That's why we give to this task and to all of our activities one hundred percent of ourselves. No matter how small the task may seem—picking up a speck of dust—or how big, we still give it one hundred percent. As it says in the *Sandokai,* "Each thing has its own intrinsic value." It is with this very same spirit of realization that we approach our work and life.

Practicing in this way, where we realize the self within the activity because the self becomes the activity, is known in Japanese as *jijuyuzammai*. When we pick up garbage, everything is being picked up. Therefore when it is our responsibility to pick it up, garbage is the most important part of our practice. Traditionally, the job of the *shuso**—the head monk or student—is to clean the toilet because even such a seemingly menial task has its intrinsic value. And when the *shuso* becomes the activity, they are unknowingly communicating that to everyone and to everything. That's what it means to work together, as opposed to working just by ourselves. We communicate through raking the paths, stacking the wood, and making the fire that heats the *sangha* house during our meals. We can see and feel the awareness behind the task. It's the ultimate Internet or World Wide Web. Everything is included in our activity, so we are all *really* doing it together.

When you strike the *bonsho,* it means that you give birth or you make a path for Buddha to appear. Before striking it in the early morning, at three-thirty or four-thirty depending on the temple, the person does full prostrations. The prostration is a five-pointed bow—you come to the ground with your right knee first, then with both knees and feet, both forearms with the palms facing up, one on each side of the head, and then the fore-

---

*The ideogram *shuso* is interesting. *Shu* means "neck" and *so* means "seat." It would be easy, therefore, to think of it as meaning the "head seat," because *shuso* is considered the first student or the senior student of the practice period. The model and example. But again the character refers to the neck, not the head. So it is pointing to something that holds the head up. When we perceive reality, we should know that there's some background supporting the foreground, something essential that we don't usually consider or that remains unseen.

head. When you prostrate, you are surrendering yourself so that all five parts of your body touch the ground. And of course because you can surrender with your body, your mind and breath are in accord.

At Sonoma Mountain, before we strike the *bonsho,* we offer three prostrations and then we strike. After the last gong has sounded, we end reverently with three more prostrations. There's a story that in one particular monastery, when the monk or nun who had the position of striking the *bonsho* offered their prostration, their forehead never touched the ground. But when you make the bow, your forehead must touch the ground. This is the practice. It is not just a meaningless ritual; like so many parts of our practice it is a body teaching that orients you toward the path of the Dharma, or toward allowing the Buddha to appear in your life. That's what you're doing. So the fact that this person didn't bow totally, touching their forehead to the ground, means that they did not give up; they did not let go of their conditioned ideas, their dualistic understanding. This not-letting-go was also communicated through the sound every time they rang the bell. Can you hear it?

Young Morita's father communicated to him that the spirit and attitude and understanding of Zen is to give yourself completely to every activity, and this is what the boy took with him to Eihei-ji. When it came time for him to strike the *bonsho,* this boy drew back the very large, loglike striker they use and struck with the inspiring and compassionate caring of his father. At that time the abbot was in his room, and he heard the sound of the bell. The sound was very good because of the boy's pure inspiration. The abbot asked his attendant to bring in the new monk who had just struck the bell, and of course he expected to see a monk enter his room, but in walked this boy.

This is how we work with each other and communicate through our activity without words, without touching, without looking, without grasping. Even without all of these, our understanding can be expressed. Please make this your practice, and you will discover the greatness behind it, your original mind ground from which real communication is expressed.

12

CONFIDENCE IN YOUR ORIGINAL NATURE

In traditional Zen spirit we don't emphasize the stages in meditation practice or anything we think we've gained. We emphasize having strong confidence in our original nature. That's the spirit of Zen, and this confidence unfolds through the cultivation of practice.

EVERY YEAR OUR Zen Center offers a special practice period known as *Ango,* which means "peaceful dwelling." This refers to a peace within each person that is so pervasive and deep that it is inconceivable. *Ango* is part of the annual training cycle traditional at Zen temples and communities. At our temple we offer *Ango* during the winter and summer seasons. We follow a very rigorous schedule during this time. We're up at four o'clock before dawn, spend the entire day in practice either bowing, sitting, working, studying, or eating in a formal style, and then go to bed after the pillow bell. When you're on this kind of schedule, something happens to you, something substantial and important. You stop thinking of the hours of the day as *your* time, and you surrender to the relentlessness of the schedule. Remember, it is said that the schedule alone is your first teacher when you enter a practice place. Since the schedule is just as relentless as your delusions, which also need energy to survive, this is one of the ways Zen helps you to transfer to your spiritual practice the energy you would ordinarily give to those delusions. In the end, your delusions are seen through.

The process is very simple. Instead of focusing on your delusions, you focus on the practice, which is to be aware of your original mind. Instead of abusing yourself with mind games, like listening to a broken record over and over again, the schedule helps you to change your orientation. You stop listening to that record and shift to something positive and beneficial that helps not only you but others as well.

During the most recent *Ango* the *shuso,* the head monk or first student who leads the practice, chose a theme from Dogen-zenji's Genjo Koan: "Thus no creature ever falls short of its own completion. Wherever it stands, it does not fail to cover the ground." This means that just as you are, with your original nature, you are complete—fully equipped. You are a fully realized person. The only thing that is required is to realize it. The depth and wisdom, your own compassion and purity, are already there within you. But you must know it's there by direct experience.

During *Ango* the repetition, lack of distraction, and attention of practice help us to shed the many layers that obscure our original nature. Since we follow the same schedule every day and everything is so structured, things that were hidden beneath the surface begin to emerge. It's a bit like being under a microscope; you begin to see a wonderful side of yourself that has always been there. And often you will see your very dark side as well. But because the practice period creates an opportunity for it to surface, you can be with it. Because you can see your dark side and be with it, you can also let it go. It's like a general house cleaning. That's one of the wonderful gifts of *Ango*.

All Asian schoolchildren are familiar with the first syllable of *Ango*. The simple ideogram *an* means "peace" or "repose." Suzuki-roshi referred to it as having to do with composure. *Re* means "again" or "return or come back to," and the other half of the word *repose* suggests calm or rest. It even means "to be dead." In Zen it's very wonderful to be dead. But what dies? In Zen practice it's your conditioned self and self-centeredness that die. When we become aware of these delusions, they begin to dissolve. Therefore you are not hindered by these obstacles. Then your true being vividly comes alive.

When you dwell in something, you take root. Dwelling means something different from living in, say, Santa Rosa or San Francisco or New York. *To dwell* means "to take root right here," like when I strike my stick against this floor: *Bam!* That's taking root. *Ango* is a period of peaceful dwelling because it has this kind of rootedness. It creates a wondrous feeling of peacefulness and dignity. You know that this is the only place you want to be right now. You're not thinking about what you're going to have for lunch, or what you're going to do after lunch, which is really just playing the same old broken record, the same abusive tape.

When you focus on practice and be where you are, something changes in your life. This is not just Buddhadharma. It is universal! It's not Buddhist, not Dharma, not Zen. These are just the names. Only when you let go of name and form and even the present can you truly be where you are. This is not just a one-time realization; it's something we have to cultivate over and over again.

While *Ango* has that kind of feeling, the word *anshin* refers to that very peace and repose within your own heart/mind. It is anchored within the Buddhadharma: an inconceivable peace that is always with you. Some of you may experience it during your sitting. In such a case it is called *anza*, "sitting in repose" or "sitting in peace," fully at ease. During *zazen* many of us sit with a lot of tension, perhaps because our understanding is new and to hold up the posture and to harmonize the breath and mind is not an easy thing to do—it takes long practice. But once they are in accord, you will actualize "sitting in repose." *Anza* is the expression of *anshin*.

I've been discussing quite a few words with you here, but I do want to mention just one more: *doan*. *Doan* means "hall practice." When you come into this meditation hall, you encounter a very peaceful feeling, but this feeling does not exist outside your body and mind. You perceive it as peaceful because you must also be peaceful. As I've said before, how can we perceive anything if we're not part of it? Integrity, wisdom, strength: The fact that we can perceive them means that we are also a part of them. The *doan* is the person who rings the bells and gongs in this hall to convey this feeling.

One time when Tomoe Katagiri-sensei was here at Sonoma Mountain teaching sewing, we had to go buy some material. My sons were with us, and we decided to have a little treat at the Burger King next to the fabric store. We had french fries and a Coke. All four of my sons were with me, which is a rare occasion, and I said, "This is one of the best moments of my life. I would not want to be anywhere else than right here." One son told me later that tears came to his eyes because he never thought that a moment could be like that. In a sense, as a practicing *sangha* we are reminding ourselves over and over again of the fact that we're tired of losing our sense of presence. The word *doan* also implies the feeling of presence, and the sound of the bell will convey it.

Even though it may be hard to imagine yourself feeling that kind of peace, it is really preciously close. It doesn't have anything to do with your age or how long you've practiced. It is not even the result of practice. In fact, we should be a little simpler and not so clever. This kind of repose has nothing to do with any of these conditions at all.

When Dogen-zenji wrote in the Genjo Koan that each of us is fully equipped, that no creature ever falls short of its own completion, that wherever it stands it does not fail to cover the ground, he was expressing the Dharma principle that we are already full of life and endowed with this life that fills us. Included in this life is everything we need, right here and right now. We are already rooted in the great peace or repose I've been discussing; this is our original nature, our Buddha Nature, beyond any circumstances or conditions that may arise.

Having confidence in our original nature is at the heart of what Suzuki-roshi called traditional Zen spirit. In traditional Zen spirit we don't emphasize the stages in meditation practice or anything we think we've gained. We emphasize having strong confidence in our original nature. That's the spirit of Zen, and this confidence unfolds through the cultivation of practice.

Most people think that if they practice for a certain number of years, they will gain enlightenment. This is not the traditional spirit of Zen. We shouldn't say, "If I sit a *sesshin* or if I do one *Ango,* I will get this," because after five, six, or seven years of practicing with this gaining idea in the back of your mind, you will be completely discouraged. A gaining idea creates karma. Suzuki-roshi always used to say, "Be careful of your gaining idea." Of course, if you have a gaining idea to benefit all sentient beings, that's a pretty good one, but the traditional Zen spirit is not to gain, not to practice for a long time, with the idea that then you will attain enlightenment. This is a big mistake. It's better to look at practice like night and day.

Right now it's daytime, but actually the stars are out. Already nighttime is here, but we can't see the stars. And day doesn't just—*ta da!*—become light. But this is how we think. We miss the wholeness of each moment and think, "This is black, and this is white, and if I practice this long, then—*ta da!*—enlightenment!" But right now if you just watch nature, you'll see that in the middle of the day there's some dark. Night is already here. I hope you see this well and understand.

As I've mentioned before, in Zen there are different schools, dealing with sudden enlightenment and gradual enlightenment. I'm supposedly from the Soto school, the gradual enlightenment way. But actually I don't really consider myself just Soto. Zen will do. You can follow your master: Be the Soto way, kind of quiet and calm and very detailed. But a shout once in a while or hitting the floor is okay, too. Anything that works is what I'm interested in. The Rinzai school is the school of sudden enlightenment. You practice, and all of a sudden—*ta da!*—you've got it! The whole thing makes me laugh because all of this is just our conditioned idea, and we fail in this area over and over again.

In actuality, what happens is like night and day. There is no sudden enlightenment. There is not even gradual enlightenment. Those are just words, like Zen dust. There have been big debates throughout Zen history. People ask, "Are you from the sudden school or the gradual school?" We shouldn't get involved in those kinds of debates. We should know through and through what is practice.

Debates like these are not in the Zen spirit because, as you can see in the quote from Dogen, even as we just begin to practice *zazen,* enlightenment is already there. It's like starting at zero when you're in a circle. You go around the circle 360 degrees, and you're back at zero. So really you don't go anywhere. You don't become any purer than you originally were. You don't become any more enlightened than you were. You just return to where you came from. So maybe some of you will want to just get off your cushions and go home right now. But in some other traditions they might say, "Well, maybe if you stay here a couple more years, you just might get it."

We think we're going to go from zero to 180 degrees all the way to 360 degrees. Wow! That's great. But actually you're already there. All you have to do is just realize it as you are. And that's you, vividly here. Where else could you be? That's the whole thrust of Zen.

During mealtime, beneath the shade of our venerable oak tree, the *shuso* spoke about chopsticks. During the meal I saw him put the ends of his chopsticks together with his fingers, and he was smiling. Then at the end of that meal he gave a little talk about the chopsticks. He said, "I think the chopsticks feel good when I put them together." It's very much like my shoes. I don't just throw them on the ground or kick them off my feet when I'm finished wearing them, because they take me everywhere. I appreciate my shoes. It's possible that if it weren't for my shoes, I wouldn't be able to get here. They help my feet, so when I take them off, I put them together. And as the *shuso* demonstrated, it's the same with the chopsticks. They help me to eat. I have regard for these insentient beings. They help me pick up food and put it in my mouth.

Things like this are a part of our enlightenment. For example, if a particular student who has a habit of always being late changes his orientation and starts being on time, that changes his whole life. It's like a container of water. If you pour a few drops of bleach into the container, it changes the whole composition. If you have difficulty being on time, and then you're on time, the whole structure of your delusion will begin to change. That's a definite part of waking up. Remember, night is already here during the daytime. Look to the small things: putting your shoes together, being on time. Don't wait for the big thing. It's the small things, all those pieces, that make the whole. There's no part without the whole, and there's no whole without the parts. Originally we are one. But in our conditioned, gaining way of thinking, we have it separated, and as a result we will always be dissatisfied. Life always seems to be moving ahead of us, and we always feel as if we are losing. It's like chasing your own shadow—you can never catch it. So in that way life, or enlightenment, is not sudden. It doesn't just happen suddenly out of nowhere. It's already happening when you do those small things.

The most important thing is to have strong confidence in your original nature, in your Buddha Nature. I hope you don't forget this. Then you won't need to spend time thinking about sudden enlightenment versus gradual enlightenment, or big enlightenment versus small enlightenment. As you practice with this confidence, it will allow what has always resided within you to emerge as you are lived by your life. And because the practice during *Ango* is so strenuous and we sit for long periods of time, your confidence is really tested. This is good because it gets to be proven over and over again. During this time, as you look at yourself more closely, you are able to see the things that have been keeping your whole self from emerging. You can allow these things to appear. Even if it feels as if they are embedded in your flesh, where each cell has a memory, they still long to surface. When they finally do appear, actively accept them, then let them go their way. Only your confidence in your original nature can help you to "just do it!" The fact remains that it's through your direct experience of your original nature that this confidence is appreciated.

13

Life of Vow: Going Straight on a Ninety-Nine-Mile Curve

The way to live depends upon our strength of vow, and our awareness of it. This will determine how we receive suffering. Buddha is very generous. He will give you lots of suffering until your capacity is filled, which makes you come to know what you must do.

OFTEN WHEN WE DISCUSS something or read about it, the subject of the discussion begins to appear bigger than it really is, and before long we think it's so far from our daily lives that we can't approach it. We project so many ideas and fears onto what we are discussing that pretty soon the thing in itself is completely obscured. With a subject like *vow*, this can easily happen. It's important to know that it is only a thought that makes it seem so distant from our lives. But the reason we practice Zen is to cultivate and confirm what we already have. That's the most important thing. And so I want to assure you that even right now *vow* is preciously close to you and always on your side.

In general, *vow* is not such a popular word. Webster's dictionary says *vow* has something to do with being solemn and making a commitment. It also mentions dignity and seriousness. Understood correctly, the word *vow* has the power to free us, because we have a karmic life—where our lives are based on our confused and dualistic understanding, driven by greed, anger, and delusion—and we also have a life of vow. The life of vow is rooted in our own steadfast awareness and intention, which are elements of the clear direction, or common denominator, that I've mentioned before. You make your choice about which life you want to live, so part of what this word really means is "wisdom-awareness."

One of the reasons many Zen students misunderstand even some pretty basic ideas is that they take the words literally and end up missing the spirit behind them. It's like when Suzuki-roshi said, "When you meet a teacher, you should leave your teacher"—quite a few people understood this literally and became confused. But he didn't mean it that way. We should remember this when studying Dharma vows. For example, about twenty years ago a student asked me, "How can we save all sentient beings?" He was referring to the first of the four great vows, "Sentient beings are numberless, I vow to save them." That's a very good question, one that endures, and many other people have asked it as well, adding, "It seems impossible. How can I make such a vow?"

There's a wonderful book called *The Collected Works of Chinul,* translated by Buswell. Chinul may be considered the Dogen of Korea. In the book he mentions ten preliminary stages on the way of the Bodhisattva's path. According to Chinul, the beginning of the path starts with faith and then progresses through other

Dharma qualities like effort, mindfulness, *samadhi,* wisdom, and protecting the Dharma. It continues until it reaches *vow*—the power of vow. Such a small word, but such a powerful one. It is said that the power of vow ignites the flame of our wisdom right in the midst of our everyday lives, so when we are reminded of our vow, simultaneously our awareness makes us go straight. Going straight is only point by point, or dot to dot, even on a ninety-nine-mile curve.

For instance, when a diver climbs the ladder to dive into a pool, the diving board may be very high, and you can imagine what is going on in his or her mind. I've never seen a diver come back down once they've reached the top, though maybe it has happened because it's just like our life. But in any case the diver has made this vow, this resolution that she's going to dive and not turn back. She climbs the ladder, rung by rung, steps onto the springboard—up, down, up, and down, then up and *off.* Even though she's been sprung from the springboard, there's still some chance that she can feel slightly off in the form. It's just that subtle. So she must remain clear and connected to her resolution or vow all the way through the dive, even after touching the water. She is the dive.

The power of vow activates your *prajna/*wisdom, your awareness, and there are so many times when we need this to happen. The Dalai Lama said once that he had a sexual dream, and in his dream—right in the middle of the dream—he said, "I am a monk."That's the power of vow coming through even in his deep sleep.

Vow is awareness that comes from our *zazen* to not repeat samsara. According to Buddhist understanding, samsara is the wheel, or merry-go-round, of life and death, including the false or conditioned views that plague all human beings. There's a difference between a life of karma, which is samsara, and a life of vow. When we live a life of samsara, a life ruled by karmic power, we have a dualistic approach to everything. We think, "I am here, and that's over there, so I am going to go from here to there. I'm going to go from here *up* to there, or from there *down* to here." One way to say it is that our mind sees everything with a subject/object, dualistic orientation. Everything is separated into parts, and no whole unites them. As you know, this creates an enormous amount of suffering.

The way to live depends upon our strength of vow, and our awareness of it. This will determine how we receive suffering. Buddha is very generous. He will give you lots of suffering until your capacity is filled, which makes you come to know what you must do. But when we come to that point, more suffering may still appear. More or less does not seem to matter. What is required is that we become aware of what's happening with our lives. This vow/awareness is an antidote to samsara. You will find this as you begin to live by vow and cultivate relinquishing those things that keep you on samsara's wheel.

Most people live a life of karma, and when you take refuge in the Dharma, you make a vow to try not to uphold the karmic life. Everyone longs to get off the wheel of samsara. That's when the vow power ignites, and that's when you assert, "I am here. I am right here. Nowhere else. I can let go of this burden in my mind." When you do, the power of vow is activated. It rises to the surface, and your conflict, your hesitation, and your doubt find their resolution. This is because a determination to do, or not to do, becomes action, but it is not just an intellectual thing. This determination, or inner commitment, is really your own wisdom, which permeates your whole body and mind.

Rather than describe it from the outside, it's better to demonstrate what vow is. Suppose I were to look straight ahead, not left, not right, just straight ahead, in a clear direction. That's vow. It's losing the self. The vow is the place where the precepts, *zazen,* and the whole philosophy intersect. In Zen everything goes to this intersection; everything returns to this intersection of the essence of mind because it is the origin. Dogen wrote, "When you leave the way to the way . . ." This word *when* has a thunderous sound to it. *When* is the exact moment when horizontal meets vertical. It's not the *when* that we think with our dualistic mind. This *when* transcends the dualistic mind. That's Zen. *When!* There's no wobbling, no hesitation. It's not something that moves from here to there. It comes from this intersection, this place of vow, where essence of mind is pervasively overflowing.

In the Dogen quote above he says, "When you leave the way to the way, you attain the way. At the time of attaining the way, the way is always left to the way." If you substitute "the way" with "zazen," you could say, "When you leave *zazen* to *zazen,* you attain *zazen.* At the time of attaining *zazen, zazen* is always left to *zazen.*" In other words, there is nothing for us to do when we are doing *zazen.* When we sit in this way we are *nondoing zazen.* This is the point. When we practice in this way, we are practicing with what Dogen calls our "whole vowlike body." We are not practicing the concept of *zazen* or some idea about it. It has to become part of this body/mind. That's the vow I'm talking about. There's no separation between "you" and the vow, "you" and *zazen,* between a bird and the sky or even a fish and water. This is something that cannot be explained; it is a very deep resolution and inner quest that we have already made. But even though we did this, we must invoke it over and over again because the power of karma and conditioning is so strong.

One very simple but important way to do this is to ask yourself, "What am I doing?" That's vow. You're asking yourself during the day, "What am I doing now?" When you ask this from the heart of vow, the word *what* has the same thunderous sound as Dogen's *when,* and it ignites the flame of wisdom right here. That's vow!

Another very simple but powerful thing you can practice is to say during the day, "I'm aware of samsara." It's like the Dalai Lama, who symbolizes the embodiment of the Bodhisattva of mercy and compassion, Avalokiteshvara. Even in the dream he said, "I am a monk." He's got good training. He usually says, "I am a simple monk." That's pretty good. If you can say it in a dream, it has become part of your body/mind. It's the same with us: "I am aware of karmic life." Because that's the awareness inside our vow. When we practice this, we can forget the self, and the power of vow will naturally strengthen and emerge. But we have to decide to do it.

The late Katagiri-roshi talked about the importance of decisiveness in relation to vow. When he was a young monk, he was frequently alone with his master, Hayashi-roshi, who was very strict. There's a period for baths that everyone usually takes together, and when he took a bath with his teacher, he always asked his teacher if he could wash his back. That's very much in their tradition. But every time he asked, "May I wash your back?" the master would say, "No!" Very short and brisk. This went on for a whole year, and it was really a koan for Katagiri. He said, "What should I do? My intention is good. I think I'm being kind." But actually he wanted some approval from his teacher. That was the extra that his teacher had sensed all this time, which is why he kept saying no whenever Katagiri-roshi asked. Finally, after one year, once again he found himself in the bath, and this time Katagiri simply got the cloth soaking wet and, without asking, went right over and began to scrub his master's back. The master said, "Uh, oh, oh, oh." It was too late. That kind of decisiveness and determination is vow. "Should I wash his back? He said to me yesterday he didn't want his back washed. Maybe he'll say that again today." All this extra baggage is a burden. Life is actually simple, but we usually carry this extra baggage, and it wears us down because of the lack of vow.

The first of the four great vows is *Sentient beings are numberless; I vow to save them.* Usually we think, "Look at all those people out there. How am I going to do it?" Just like the student who asked me the question. It is the conditioned mind, the karmic or dualistic mind, that thinks this way—how in the world can we save all those people out there?

The second vow is *Desires are inexhaustible; I vow to put an end to them.* How am I going to put an end to all my desires, even the desire to live? Isn't it natural to want to live? Do I have to give that up, too?

The third and fourth vows are *The Dharmas are boundless; I vow to master them* and *The Buddha's way is unsurpassable; I vow to attain it.*

These are the four Bodhisattva vows, and some of the difficulties you'll naturally encounter in your life in relation to them.

When you first encounter the first vow, you might reasonably ask what it means to deliver an infinite number of sentient beings. A quote from the Sixth Ancestor, Hui Neng's Platform Sutra, may clarify this. It says, "It does not mean that I, Hui Neng, am going to deliver them. I, Hui Neng, include the ten thousand beings." Then the sutra continues, "And who are these sentient beings within our mind?" This is the key right here—who are these sentient beings within our mind? I am and you are. We are the beholder of all these sentient beings. "They are the delusive mind, the deceitful mind, the evil mind, and suchlike minds—all these are sentient beings." All these are just delusive thoughts that create the illusion of our separate world. This is what we are going to be saved or delivered from, right here within ourselves. In our investigation we will reveal that behind each delusion there is nothing. This is the ground of our realization, and so we exclaim: The sky is blue and the grass is green! Originally, ancient Buddhas always stated that the Dharma is the mind of sentient beings.

When the Sixth Ancestor says, later on, that we have to deliver ourselves by our own essence of mind, how are we to do it? We do it through our *samadhi,* we focus on this eternal essence by turning our light inward without the gaining mind. That's the basic point, and that is what it means to save all sentient beings. When this is *realized* and continually cultivated with our awareness (there's that *when* again) and you are in the world, you will discover that your relationship to each sentient being has changed. You may not be overwhelmed by the situations you find yourself in, because *those* sentient beings are also *this* sentient being. It's like a mother and child. The child is not separate from the mother. But in our karmic life we've separated everything. In the *life of vow* we cannot separate because they are all a part of us and we are exactly a part of them, whether we like it or not.

It is through the essence of mind, which is unborn, indestructible, calm, and clear, that we deliver ourselves within ourselves. This is the basic reality of Dharma. It's not your teacher who is going to deliver you; through the practice you're going to deliver yourself within yourself. That's the power of vow, but we have to be willing to climb up the ladder onto the diving board (though actually having been born means that we're already on the board). The only thing to do then is to dive whole-heartedly, to jump right in. That's delivering ourselves by cultivating our own essence of mind. And that's the vow of saving all sentient beings. Going straight, point by point, dot to dot, on a ninety-nine-mile curve.

14

LEAVES FALL

These signs of falling apart are actually wholesome signs,
and it is at great cost that we avoid what nature is
repeatedly teaching.

BEFORE EACH DHARMA talk at the Zen Center, we chant the following verse:

The Dharma, incomparably profound and infinitely subtle,
Is rarely met even in a hundred, thousand, million kalpas.*
Now we see it, hear it, receive, and maintain it.
May we completely realize the Tathagata's true meaning.

This opening chant may seem kind of heavy, but actually it's a chant about the most intimate part of our true nature. It doesn't mean that "I" will give a perfect Dharma talk and that you

---

*As I mentioned, a *kalpa* is an immeasurable length of time, sometimes compared to an aeon. Suppose a heavenly deity descended from the sky once every hundred years and lightly brushed the side of Sonoma Mountain with the sleeves of her robes. When she finally wore the mountain down, that would be one *kalpa*.

will "get it." It's not like that at all. The talk is an attempt to create a mirror so you may see who you are, or what your original nature is, in spite of all the difficulties you may experience in your life. Just how you actually are. It's like the Japanese word *sonomama*, which means "as it is." It means seeing our everyday world without greed, anger, or ignorance. Since this is at the core of our training and practice, little by little you are training and practicing "as it is."

The ancient ideogram for *practice* is like a crossroads, an intersection. When you're at this threshold, you don't know exactly what's going to happen. Isn't that true? *Crossroads* is a good word for it. In practice, you're being suspended in space at this crossroads. Dharma students, and especially Zen students, use the term *practice* a great deal. I feel it's overused, but Dogen defined *practice* as giving life to your original self. This is not giving life to your deluded self, which we do all the time, but to your original self, to your basic goodness, or you could say to your Buddha Nature, which each one of us intrinsically possesses whether we realize it or not. This is the word *practice*. It can be understood in a very oceanic way or in a very shallow way, but still practice is always practice, and its truth is to ignite and reveal your true self within your everyday life.

You may do part of this in small ways, like arriving for your appointment on time or getting out of bed as soon as you wake up. For some people it might be learning to say no; for others, saying yes. They are small things to ignite your true self, or to assert your position and not move from it. Perhaps we can say that in practice we make an unconditional vow to not give up on ourselves. This is the vow, no matter what happens, and the physical practice is the means by which we manifest this vow.

As I say this, it is the season of Thanksgiving. Giving thanks may be one of the best American traditions that we have. Year upon year, when I walk back to my home after morning *zazen* during this fall season, I still feel touched by the landscape, the subtle richness of this whole environment. In recent years our neighbors have planted more grapes, so that by now, as we move through this season, the vineyard has turned to an infinite rolling field of yellow, orange, and magenta. Because the vines are spent, we can really appreciate the great teacher nature is in all its splendor.

What do you think when you see these vines? When I look at them, it reminds me that we should let things fall, as trees let their leaves fall. I don't know what kind of tree you would be if you could choose; maybe all of your leaves would hold on and never fall off. Maybe that's your kind of tree. Some trees keep their leaves, or needles, because they are evergreen and that's just their nature. But if we were a maple, we would shed our autumn leaves. We would naturally let them fall. It is said that at the moment when the person Gautama became Shakyamuni Buddha (the moment of his realization under the *bodhi* tree), all of its leaves began to fall to the great earth. It must have been a thunderous sight. Maybe some leaves had already fallen and some still held on while he sat there, but it is said that when he attained realization, all of the leaves fell off. It's beautifully symbolic in the sense that realization, or seeing your Buddha Nature *as it is* is not about holding on to things but about naturally letting them fall.

Our usual way is to say "God, I'm falling apart. My arm, my thumb don't work as well as they used to, and sometimes my knee." But these signs of falling apart are actually wholesome signs, and it is at great cost that we avoid what nature is repeatedly teaching. Every season there's a Dharma within a Dharma. We don't have to wait for spring because there is also an eternal spring. There is an eternal fall. Our seasons are eternal, and they are right here in our fingertips, right here within ourselves. So really it is always a time for thanks and giving, for appreciation of our lives.

The late Maezumi-roshi always encouraged everybody to appreciate their life. To appreciate something, you have to be present. You cannot see beauty as something just outside yourself, so being present means being beauty itself. Then your appreciation will naturally deepen. When I think of all of Dogen's extraordinary teachings in his Genjo Koan in this way, it makes me want to tell you that "Appreciate your life" could be a translation for the whole Genjo Koan. In order to know how to appreciate your life, you have to know something about life and death, gain and loss. Here is a fragrant but very beautiful and profound section from the Genjo Koan that will help you to understand and appreciate life as it is:

Firewood turns into ash and does not turn into firewood again. But do not suppose that ash is after and firewood before. We must realize that firewood is in a state of being firewood and it has its before and after. Yet despite this past and future, its present is independent of them. Ash is in a state of being ash and it has its before and after. Just as firewood does not become firewood again after it is ash, so after one's death one does not become alive again. Thus that life does not become death is an unqualified fact of the Buddha Dharma. For this reason, life is called the nonborn. That death does not become life is the Buddha's revolving of the confirmed Dharma wheel, therefore death is called the nonextinguished. Life is a period of itself. Death is a period of itself. For example, they are like winter and spring. We do not think that winter becomes spring. Nor do we say that spring becomes summer.

This is none other than ourselves. We are the firewood. We are the ash. After we turn into ash, we don't become firewood again. Each thing has its own beingness. Firewood is in a state of being firewood, just like your self is in a state of being your self. And right now this present moment contains its before and after. No matter how we think about it, the past has already gone, what we call "after" has not yet arrived, and we don't even know where the present is, because it's continuously changing. Everything is in a state of flux.

These are the falling leaves. Everything is changing. In one way it's complete freedom. It is said that there are 6.5 billion instances in twenty-four hours. And in one second there are seven thousand instances. As we are sitting here they are continuously coming and continuously going, just like when I strike my stick on the floor: *Bam-bam-bam-bam-bam.* Isn't that wonderful? This is complete freedom. We see ourselves as firewood going to ash. We see ourselves thirty years old, going to sixty. "My God, look out, here comes seventy!" We see ourselves only in the linear, the sequential, moving toward an end. We don't understand that within each twenty-four-hour day there are 6.5 billion instances of life, death, life, death, gain, loss, gain, loss, dark, light, Bodhisattvas, clouds, cars, you, and me. All the dharmas are appearing and disappearing continually out of the beginningless beginning and the endless end. This is really fantastic. It gives us such a very wide, liberating view that to even call it Buddhadharma or anything else diminishes it.

Ash is in the state of being ash. As ash, it has its before and after, its past and future. But just as firewood does not become firewood again, after it is ash, after we're dead, we don't have a second chance. This is the only chance we have, right here, right now. "Thus," Dogen writes, "life does not become death." Our lives are not sequential. Our lives are not conditional. Life does not become death. This "is an unqualified fact of the Buddha Dharma," and "for this reason, life is called the nonborn," or the unborn. "That death does not become life is the Buddha's revolving of the confirmed Dharma wheel, therefore death is called the nonextinguished." The nonborn, the nonextinguished. Therefore, life is a period of itself. We have to appreciate this. Life is a period of itself, and death is also a period of itself. They cannot be avoided, because we all are faced with them over and over again. Probably the things you fear most will happen. What is it for you? For most people it is death. But if you fear death, you fear life, being *engaged* in life. I was a slow learner. Even with Zen practice, it took me fifty, sixty years to begin, to not be preoccupied, not self-concerned, not dreaming, not spaced out, but to be engaged in life.

Not to be preoccupied. *Preoccupied* means "this space is already taken." And that's what happens, isn't it? But life passes swiftly, and we only have this one chance. As Dogen says, "Death does not become life again." So even if you're afraid in the situation, just say it, don't deny it. Right when you begin to feel yourself shaking inside, and little by little you become aware and recognize the fear, go ahead and say it: "Yes, I am afraid." That releases you back into life, that's the falling of the leaf that makes it possible for you to be engaged in life right where you are.

And that's the real Thanksgiving. The turkey and abundance of food are an expression of this truth; they are the real nourishment of appreciating your life so that it can also be Thanksgiving every day. When I am really alive, I needn't *try* to be present in all the 6.5 billion instances a day. I am just here. I see the leaves fall in spite of my noisy, chattering mind. And at the same time I can hear the birds pecking on the roof of the *zendo* because this person, this Dharma, *as it is,* includes everything. It's a way of being that is soft and flexible, and so generous. This is the magnanimous life!

15

INTIMATE STUDY

Intimacy itself is at the heart of all of Zen. When we are intimate with anything, or with everything, we are simultaneously being intimate with ourselves.

AN IMPORTANT PART of Zen practice is study. Of course, we study the self through meditation and other activities, but we also study the world, as well as some of the abundant and profound literature that has come out of Zen practice. In each of these ways we are always studying the self. It is a big mistake to think that when we read writings on the lives of some of our ancestors, we're studying about someone besides ourselves, because each phrase, letter, and even the space between the letters is actually pointing toward ourselves. This is the underlying meaning of what we call intimate study. Actually, we might say that intimacy itself is at the heart of all of Zen. When we are intimate with anything, or with everything, we are simultaneously being intimate with ourselves.

Early dawn, when the sky is clear, I can see the stars from my bed. It feels so peaceful and quiet with these bright beings pulsating through the universe. When we're small, we're taught that the sky is over there, far away, so the parents and children feel that they have some idea of where the sky is. But maybe that should be only the beginning idea and parents should also say to their children, "You are part of that sky, and that sky is part of you." In this way parents would be introducing their children to intimacy with the world.

In Buddhism there are many theories and formulas, many ways of understanding reality through the wisdom of experience that are very true. They are not just speculation. For nearly twenty-six hundred years they have been tested and proven, which is what makes them so profound. We see the sky, but because we see it with our conditioned eyes and mind, we believe the sky is quite distant, that it is only "over there" and so the sky is not a part of us anymore. It is the same for the flowers, the trees, and the ground we stand on; all of those "objective" things. But who is it who sees the sky? That's the most important question. If you can see the sky, you must be part sky, otherwise you couldn't see it. Isn't that true? If you see anger, you are part anger also. At our Zen Center we have a kind of formula that we chant in the Heart Sutra every day that expresses this: Form is emptiness. These words mean that *this* form, *this* subject, or *this* person is *that* sky. We are inseparable. When you place your hand over your heart, you are also touching the sky.

The mirror side of this formula, form is emptiness, is that emptiness is also form. This means that not only are we the sky but simultaneously we are ourselves as well. Basically, this is our first realization: Form is emptiness, emptiness is form. In Zen this is one of the ways we express this intimacy.

When we allow ourselves to see through the transparency of our conditioned self, then those things that we think are not a part of us, like the sky, the flower, the tree, the leaves, may become our-selves. And when we do come to experience this, it is one of life's greatest gifts of intimacy. Once this has become part of us, we can really understand that it is also true that I am *this* person, *this* form, and likewise that the sky is a manifestation in form known as the sky. So we have both: The sky is emptiness, or infinite space, and at the same time the sky is bound by the sky. I am emptiness, and I am I. Knowing this makes the difference in how we see and live our very own precious lives.

On the back cover of *Cultivating the Empty Field*—which is based on the life of the great Chinese Zen master Wanshi Shogaku, who lived in China from 1091 to 1157—the late Maezumi-roshi from Zen Center of Los Angeles wrote, "Wanshi is one of those few Chinese masters who have had a profound influence on the Japanese Soto Zen tradition. The 'Silent Illumination' expounded in his *Extensive Record* is that the tongueless one prescribes (with wordless sparklings) a medicine of the nondual existence for the bodiless ones. The mouthless ones take it and rejoice in lives free from illness. When we appreciate the effect of this medicine, we know that Master Wanshi's 834-year-old relics are still fresh and warm and vitally universal."

This is very powerful: tongueless, wordless, bodiless—and we, the mouthless ones, who take this medicine and rejoice in lives free from illness. When I first read this, I thought of the late Suzuki-roshi and His Holiness XVI Karmapa having cancer but, at the same time, being free from illness. Do you understand? They had cancer and they died from cancer, but they were also free from illness because of the faith they had experienced through their authentic practice, faith based on the "medicine of the nondual existence."

When life is experienced this way, when you are sick you are just sick; that's being free from illness. We don't worry if we're going to die, or not die, if we have some deep understanding of what death actually is. Not personal death, but universal death.

Please don't die if you think your life and death are just your own, or if you believe you're ready to die just for yourself. Please don't die yet, because this universal self includes the moon, the stars and sky, all of your friends, brothers and sisters, and even people you don't like. It includes everything.

This kind of universal death is important to understand and to know. I imagine many people think they're ready to die, and they actually die. But it's a very small, insignificant, divided death, one separated from everything in the universe. This was my own experience when I had cancer in the spring of 1976. I thought I was ready. Just before I slept each night, I felt I was coming closer to the gate of death. I would say to myself, "I think I'm ready."

Now I realize how foolish and ignorant I was. My misunderstanding didn't include the moon, the stars, the sky, my wife and four sons, my students and friends. Embarrassingly enough, this was true even though I had been sitting *zazen* for sixteen years. Fortunately, I realized how much work I had to do; it was a very close call.

I'm sad to say I feel that many people, also because of their ignorance, die in this insignificant and limited way, as opposed to the universal way that includes everything. But there really is no need to resist meeting death with this open attitude. We all long to return to the spaciousness from where we come, or to which we are born, moment after moment. This is pure intimacy— seeing *things as it is*—or through and through.

When Maezumi-roshi uses the words "tongueless," "bodiless," and "mouthless," he's taking the usual meaning away from these objective things. This is really a wonderful sentence: "The mouthless ones take this medicine, which is wordless sparklings spoken with no tongues." "Tongue" refers to our conditioning, but "tongueless" means without conditioning, so it has no beginning and no end. This is the real foundation of silent illumination. And because the self includes the sky and all things, each of us is the mouthless one who takes the medicine of the nondual and who rejoices in life free from illness.

Does it make sense to you that when you see a flower, or when you see beauty, at that very moment you must be beauty? I hope so, because it means that beauty is not outside of yourself; you are beauty, and you are truth. We can appreciate the beauty of a flower because we also feel its impermanence as our own. We can say we know that roses and thorns are as inseparable as night and day because it is no different with us. It *is* us. Therefore, beholding the flower, or carefully holding the rose, we can treasure our own beauty and appreciate the evanescence of this fleeting life.

In your *zazen* practice you will see the thinking mind spin, spin, spin, and the Big Mind will just watch it spin. That may be something new for some of you, and it's a very interesting phenomenon. The Big Mind will watch it, but since its nature is immovable, it won't spin with it. This reminds me of the poem by Wanshi in which he alludes to the empty nature and function of this Big Self. The last four lines are very beautiful, and each one sparkles like the separate facets of one translucent diamond. These lines come from Wanshi's poem "Acupuncture Needle of *Zazen*":

> The water is clear right down
> to the bottom.
> Fish swim lazily on.
> The sky is vast without end.
> Birds fly far into the distance.

There was another Chinese Zen master who was called Stone Head because he sat on a very large stone and that is where he would meditate. Some of you may know that Stone Head was none other than Sekito Kisen, who wrote the *Sandokai*, the *Intimacy of the One and Many*. While sitting like a stone one day, Sekito experienced an awakening while recalling the words "The ultimate person is empty and hollow." Form is emptiness, emptiness is form, the ultimate person is empty and hollow, tongueless, bodiless, wordless, mouthless, empty, and hollow. "He or she has no form, yet in the myriad things there is none that is not their own making. Who can understand the myriad things as oneself? Only the sage." Sekito Kisen is saying that sages *realize* they have "no self," yet there is nothing that is not themselves.

We must become familiar with this inherent essence of emptiness and hollowness. Every night when we go to sleep, we slip into unconsciousness. We enter into the dark every evening, and it's really surprising, when you think about it, that even without an alarm clock you can wake up from your sleep. That is a pretty fantastic phenomenon. From our sleep we can wake up, and so in exactly the same way, whether we are in the middle of the night hours or midday, we wake up from our delusion.

Wanshi was a very bright young man, and at a very early age he memorized six or seven thousand Chinese characters, which is a very difficult feat. His father was a lay practitioner, and it is said that his father's teacher predicted that Wanshi would one day become "a vessel of the Dharma," meaning one who realizes and teaches the Dharma. When Wanshi was eleven years old, he left home and became a monk. He studied under a Zen master by the name of Kumu. *Ku* is "dry," and *mu* is "wood," and this person practiced sitting meditation in a manner that was so still that his body resembled a block of dry wood. This is bodiless, mouthless, tongueless, wordless. The thoughts in your mind don't activate, and you have no interest in your thinking mind, yet you are vividly alive.

We must find some other perspective on the thinking mind. We must see that there is a clear-thinking and an unclear-thinking mind. The unclear-thinking mind constantly works on you; its seemingly infinite life span will wear you out and will confuse and mislead you. In fact, we could say that that's its attribute, and it exhibits it well. But we should try not to believe what it says, because too much unclear thinking is a kind of illness. Clear thinking lasts a very short period of time, but as you know, this other thinking goes on and on and on. You really must try to see through it, or it will take your life, it will keep you in illness so that you cannot enjoy life free from illness, because you actually believe in it.

In Wanshi's poem he is implying that Zen is basically seeing your true nature and how it functions. When your mind and body allow your original calm and stillness to emerge, your nature will appear. That's the purpose of sitting, and it's especially the purpose of long sittings, which exhaust both the thinking mind and the body until your true nature appears. And when it does, you will know that your nature is just like the water in Wanshi's poem, clear right down to the bottom. Your nature is hollow and empty through and through. When you rediscover this, you will see that a fish swims like a fish, and that the sky is vast with no end. Your nature too, just like the sky, is vast without end; it is bodiless, mouthless, wordless, tongueless. The *function* of this sky, vast without end, or the function of this water, clear right down to the bottom, is simply that a fish swims like a fish and a bird flies far into the distance. It is what is frequently referred to as the nature of the world.

We already know this ourselves. When we sit, we hold our hands in what is called the "cosmic mudra" position. This cosmic mudra symbolizes the universe, so our sitting is not so much a personal sitting, because personal sitting arises from the conditioned self or the small, exclusive self. If when we sit we remember to place our mind in the left palm, then we are placing it in the universe, in the cosmos, and therefore we are the universe. This is a good way to touch your mind. Put your mind in the palm of your left hand, and rest that palm against your *tanden,* three fingers' width below the navel, which is the power spot of your body. Practicing this also connects you to the universe as you breathe through your mudra, through the shrine it makes resting there. It is like an umbilical cord connected to the universe. Then your nostrils breathe with the spirit of Wanshi and all the ancients from the past who have brought forward this practice, this Way, and this life that is free from illness. Without clouds before them, and with your body settled majestically like a mountain, your eyes see clearly. Just practice in this way, and you will find there is nothing in any world more intimate.

16

Taking the
Backward Step

*Zazen practice is a simple and direct thing. When you give
attention to the small mind, it grows and grows and grows.
When you give attention to Big Mind, you cultivate Big
Mind. Our origin is Big Mind, so it has the spirit of giving
you the inspiration you need. Big Mind is the only thing
you can rely on.*

SHORTLY AFTER DOGEN RETURNED to Japan from his
studies in China, he wrote the *Fukanzazenji*, which may be
translated as the *Universal Promotion of the Principles or Art of
Zazen*. In this text he writes, "You should stop the intellectual
practice of pursuing words and learn the 'stepping back' of 'turning the light around and shining back'; mind and body will naturally 'drop off' and the 'original face' will appear. The Zen 'art' of
looking into the mind source instead of pursuing thoughts or
external stimuli is called *eko hensho*, 'Turning the light around and
shining [or looking] back.'"

Stepping back or *the backward step* is a very interesting phrase.
What does it mean to you? How do we initiate it and experience
it in the *zendo* as well as outside the meditation hall in our every-

day life so that we are practicing what Dogen calls "the Dharma of the sages"? Dogen points the way when he says that we take the backward step by turning our thinking mind, with the light of awareness, on our own mind source.

In our meditation practice it is very important not to become lost entertaining the thinking mind, because the activity and capacity of the thinking mind is endless. If you give it all of your attention, it will take your life. It's the same for each and every one of us: The more attention you give it, the stronger it becomes. And the more you try not to entertain it, the more you confirm its presence. Either way, it's got you. The antidote is really a very simple thing; instead of putting all of the emphasis on your small mind, put the emphasis on your Big Mind. "Cultivate your Big Mind," as Suzuki-roshi said. And so in *zazen* the backward step is taken when you turn your light of awareness inward like a mirror on your mind source.

If you hold a mirror in front of you, it will help you to straighten up—not in the sense that there is something wrong with you—but it will help you to sit up straight both physically and mentally. It will give you courage, and ultimately when you allow this light of awareness to shine on yourself, you will have your own realization.

One time at Tassajara Suzuki-roshi was ill and told his attendant to bring a very large stone, one that weighed more than thirty pounds. When this was done, he told his attendant to put the stone on top of his chest while he was lying in bed. So the *jisha* did this, and when the large stone was settled there, Suzuki-roshi said, "This stone is more real than what I'm thinking about. It's *heavy*."

After we finished building the fence in the parking lot at Sonoma Mountain, I told this story and asked the students to each bring a stone and put it underneath the fence because the stone they would carry was more real than the thoughts they were carrying in their heads. These thoughts are just fabrications, and of course we all know that the story, the human drama, goes on and on and on until it consumes our entire lives. We invest in the story, we get wrapped up in it and lost in it and then we build on it. But what is it, after all? It's really nothing. To make matters worse, as someone once said, most of the things we think about, or worry about happening, do not happen. I think it's more beneficial to carry a heavy stone and put it under the fence than to carry all this fabrication that will take our lives.

On the stupa post at Trungpa's shrine here on the mountain there is a poem by the Third Ancestor that says, "The light of the jewel illuminates the jewel itself." Isn't that a wonderful line? But this is not just Sunday poetry; it is a realization experience expressed through poetry. So when you sit—again, Zen sometimes is called silent illumination—it's not just your own sitting that's taking place. You are receiving and illuminating this light even as you sit. A jewel—for instance a diamond, which is one of the hardest things in the world yet transparent—sparkles and shines. It's brilliant. Each shining facet makes the bright jewel. And as it's shining—like your *zazen*—this illumination shines through your delusions, all the way through, illuminating the jewel itself, which is nothing other than you. This turning the light of awareness on yourself is taking the backward step.

Dogen's *Shobogenzo* is about ninety-five volumes of saying over and over again "You are Buddha" in ninety-five different ways. *Sho* means "right." The ideogram for *sho* is written in such a way that it has a sense of uprightness. Of the five strokes that constitute this ideogram, one central vertical stroke stands upright on a strong horizontal stroke. This "right" is not opposed to wrong but carries with it a sense of perfect balance and composure, so it represents uprightness instead of righteousness. *Bo* means "Dharma." *Shobo* means "right Dharma" or "true Dharma." *Gen* means "eye;" and *zo* means "treasury."

Sometime after the Buddha attained enlightenment, he went before a large assembly. A couple of hundred people were in attendance waiting for the Buddha's Dharma that day, but all he did was to hold up a flower. No one knew how to react, what to think or say, but one of those in attendance, Mahakashyapa, saw the Buddha holding a flower, and he smiled. When the Buddha saw him smile, he said, "I have the subtle teaching of the treasury of the True Dharma Eye, the wondrous mind of nirvana, the true form of no form. It does not rely on words and is transmitted outside of the scriptures. Now I entrust it to Mahakashyapa."

This is where the title of the *Shobogenzo* comes from. Part of it is rooted in the fact that Bodhidharma frequently said that the true Dharma is not dependent on words or what is written in the scriptures. It's outside the scriptures, outside our conditioned or dualistic efforts of mind. It's outside of what we think it is but not outside ourselves.

It's a pretty lofty, subtle teaching, and yet believe it or not, all this is just a description of your own mind, your own original mind. *I have the subtle teaching.* Subtle means you can't really grasp it. You can't name it. You can't see it. Subtle. It's not in front. It's in the back where you can't see it—the subtle teaching. *Of the treasury of the True Dharma Eye:* One eye is absolute, or empty, and the other eye is the relative, the phenomenal eye. The two eyes working together see one thing. One eye is emptiness; the other eye is form. But two eyes see just one thing. So the true form of no form is when Buddha holds up the flower. Nothing is said. No thought is communicated. No feeling—just holding the flower. The true form of no form. *This* does not rely on words or letters and is transmitted outside the writings or sutras. When Buddha held up the flower and saw Mahakashyapa smile, he knew that he completely understood, and so he said, "Now I entrust it to Mahakashyapa." And then, most likely, tears streamed down both of their faces.

In some temples, even here in America, a ceremony is performed called *segaki*. *Se* means "offering," and *gaki* means "hungry ghost." One way of understanding this is that during the ceremony you make an offering to the deceased people you knew and also to the deceased people who were unknown to you. But every time we do a ceremony, all of the participants must realize that we need it the most. It's not just about something or someone else, it's about ourselves. *Segaki* is about the hungry ghosts that are within ourselves.

In the wheel of samsara there are six realms. One is the realm of the hungry ghosts; one is the heavenly beings and *devas;* then there's the human realm, which we are in (actually we've visited all of the realms at one time or another); then the hell realm of eternal suffering; the realm of the animal spirits; and the realm of the fighting spirits. As we look at the mandalas and paintings of the wheel of samsara that have been created for nearly twenty-six hundred years, it's a big relief to see that there's a little Buddha in each realm. This means that freedom is only found directly within each realm of suffering. That's how we are released from the six realms, through the Buddha who is already there. It's important to know in which realm we mostly dwell.

The beings in the realm of the hungry ghosts have extremely small throats, the size of a needle. That's the width of their throats, and their bellies are very big and bloated because they are starving to death. This hungry ghost is in extreme need, a need that can never be satisfied. This is the worst thing and is manifested by many forms of greed: greed for food, for money, for sleep or sex, for material or even spiritual possessions, for attention. The very form of this hungry ghost doesn't allow it to ever be satisfied. And yet since we are human beings, it is very important to know how to be satisfied.

The story of how the *segaki* ceremony started is that Ananda, who was the Third Ancestor after Buddha, as well as being his cousin, was practicing *zazen* one day when an emaciated hungry ghost appeared before him. It really looked horrible and was extremely frightening. Ananda was startled and shocked to have it appear, because he thought his practice was pretty good. This hungry ghost stood in front of him for quite some time until it finally said, "In three days all your good karma will be void. You've had some good karma, but in three days it will all be gone. Then you will join our order." Can you imagine that?

Ananda jumped up and went to see Shakyamuni Buddha and said, "I have this terrible problem," and he told Buddha what the hungry ghost said. But it turns out that in a previous life the Buddha had consulted Kannon with the same problem, and she taught him what to do and how to handle the situation. "Make an offering," she said. Make an offering to the hungry ghost. Offer food, offer water. And that's what we do when we eat *oryoki** lunch. We offer food for the hungry ghost, but we need to know that that very hungry ghost is within ourselves. It's

---

*The offering to the hungry ghosts during *oryoki* lunch (again, *oryoki* means "just the right amount") consists of placing a small portion of food on the end of one of the utensils *(setsu)*. This offering of "just the right amount" is meant to acknowledge and satisfy our hungry ghost. What is the right amount?

some aspect of our own being. Often it manifests as an urge that does not know how to be satisfied, and our usual way is to do everything we can to try to satisfy its hunger and demands. But that's where we get caught. By continually trying to satisfy it in the usual way, we actually become its slave. That is, until we become aware of the real dynamic. Once we are aware of it, and the realm of samsara we've been in, our practice is to make an offering on behalf of it. In this way we don't seek to banish it, but we acknowledge it, we make a place for it. This awareness and action open the way for satisfaction. And of course the ultimate offering we can make is to raise the *bodhi* mind through the practice of *eko hensho*, turning the light of awareness on our own mind.

You can make an offering of this kind every day. For example, you can offer your *zazen*. There are thousands of opportunities and ways for you to make an offering on behalf of the hungry ghosts. But be careful: You don't want to get lost in it, like getting lost in your small or thinking mind. One way you can think about your small mind, because its never-ending activity is so exhaustive, is that it's a bit like a hungry ghost. It too can never be completely satisfied. But remember, the more attention you give to a hungry ghost, the stronger it becomes. And the more you try not to give it attention, the more you confirm its presence. So in order to take care of it and not be consumed, the simple offering of *eko hensho* is enough.

My deepest wish is that, somehow, wherever we are, each one of us will do something that will enable us to become fully satisfied in our life. Since no matter where we go our mind comes with us, our mind needs training in some kind of practice. This is very clear. Our dualistic, deluded thinking mind makes this clear; hungry ghosts make this clear. It doesn't matter where you practice as long as you have a practice, a strong practice, because *that* mind is equally strong. It's really true. There are many hungry ghosts inside the *zendo,* outside the *zendo,* near the *zendo,* far from the *zendo.* They show up everywhere, like on All Souls' Day or Halloween. So a strong and continuous practice is really needed. Even after realization it's still needed.

When writing about Buddha's realization, Keizan-zenji wrote a poem that is included in *The Record of Transmitting the Light* in which he said something very puzzling:

> *A splendid branch issues from the old plum tree*
> *In time, obstructing thorns flourish everywhere.*

With the plum blossom comes the thorns. With the rose there are naturally thorns. These obstructing thorns flourish everywhere. But that's the very place where it happens for you; that obstruction is the place of realization. So whether you go out or you go in, be aware. There are thorns everywhere. Don't walk too fast or too slow. They're everywhere: thorns from the old plum tree.

In order for us to meet these thorns, these ghosts, this dualistic thinking mind, we should practice in a way that has some spirit behind it, the spirit of the treasury of the True Dharma Eye. Then we don't have to worry about whether we do everything exactly right. When you practice in a way that is rooted in this spirit, that cultivates this spirit in all aspects of your life, and that gives you access to your own spirit, then this spirit will carry you through. The mind can't carry you through, you know. But practice rooted in this spirit can. And other people will see it and confirm it. It's the spirit with which a life is lived that people find so moving: how things are picked up and put down, how they are arranged, how deep the hole is dug when working in the garden, what shape it is, how our utensils are placed on the table. There's a spirit to it, just as there's a spirit to your sitting that is very important. Where does it come from?

Zazen practice is a simple and direct thing. When you give attention to the small mind, it grows and grows and grows. When you give attention to Big Mind, you cultivate Big Mind. Our origin is Big Mind, so it has the spirit of giving you the inspiration you need. Big Mind is the only thing you can rely on. Then you don't have to worry, or become obsessed with ideas of gaining and attaining, with grasping for that one special thing to satisfy you or to save your life, even transmission of the True Dharma Eye.

Once when discussing transmission a student asked me, "Can we grasp transmission?" I told him, "Maybe not in how you say it." I said this because at the moment when transmission occurs, you *are* transmission. So it's not like grasping something; there's nothing to grasp at all. How can you grasp nothingness? So you're just open to *receive*. The treasury eye is open. Whatever appears in front of it is seen, just like a mirror. When green appears before a mirror, the mirror reflects green. So you should sit there, and whatever comes in front of you, *that's it,* without any interpretation, without any projection, because there is no benefit whatsoever to these projections and interpretations; quite the opposite, they really squeeze the life out of us. There are so many thoughts about so many things that separate us from our lives and divide us from everything that is already right here. So nongrasping, nongrasping, just open your eyes and turn your light of awareness inward on your mind. That's the treasure within itself!

17

ACTIVE PARTICIPATION IN LOSS

*Accepting things as they are is a loss. Being in the moment
is a loss. We are losing every moment of our lives. What are
we losing? We are losing our self-centeredness, our self-
clinging, our ideas, our conditioning.*

IN THE LATE Uchiyama-roshi's book *Opening the Hand of
Thought,* he uses a phrase that made a very deep impression
on me because it points to something that's been part of my
life for a long time. The phrase is "active participation in loss."
Usually we want to avoid loss at all costs. We are conditioned to
seek only gain, to be happy and to try to satisfy all our desires.
Even though we understand intellectually that loss is the very
mud in our lives that the lotus needs in order to bloom, when it
comes to our actual lives, most people still believe loss is the
opposite of gain.

We are actively participating in loss. *Actively* means that we are
willing, committed, not giving up, and that we have the courage
to die while being alive. The word *loss* refers to death and all the
things we usually don't want to talk about. It also implies failure

and impermanence. It's about suffering, fear, surrender, and letting go—all those things we believe to be negative despite the fact that they actually serve as the impetus for most of us to practice. Loss in life brings us to practice. Impermanence brings us to practice. These are the perfect antidotes to a self-centered, gaining life. In fact, if we could have a very permanent or secure, guaranteed life, if that were at all possible, most people would not practice because they would feel no need.

Near the end of the fall 1991 Tokubetsu *sesshin* led by Narazaki-roshi at Tassajara Monastery, I twisted my ankle while I was saying good-bye to a group of teachers, aggravating an old injury. And then, like a fool, I stood on it. I felt the pain grip my leg and should have sat down but instead I stood there waving good-bye. Good-bye to me! The group had to catch a plane, so I wanted them to be able to leave quickly and not have to pay attention to my ankle.

After their van was out of sight, I limped back to the cabin and saw that my foot was already very swollen. I walked around with a stick, and in the evening I was surprised by the amount of pain. It took me a long time just to walk around the bed, using my hands for support. For many nights I was in agony. It felt as if I were being pulled deep underwater. It turns out that spraining and damaging a ligament or tendon is worse than breaking a bone, and in the end I had to use crutches for four months, which presented me with certain problems. For example, how would I come into the *zendo,* and once there how would I sit? How would I offer incense and bow before the altar? How would I lead the service, greet my students or visitors? There were many things to consider due to this loss of ability to do things in my usual way.

Usually we want to look as if we're in control. But my form

now had to include crutches. As I entered the *zendo,* the crutches creaked on the wooden floor. Also, I couldn't sit in full lotus as I always had done. One of my students loaned me a beach chair. I put it on my mat, but to tell the truth, part of me was afraid someone from Sotoshu Headquarters would arrive unexpectedly and see me sitting California Zen in a beach chair. I had to extend my right foot and learn how to sit again—not as I wanted to sit but as I *had* to sit. In other words, I had to do it with loss. Isn't this a wonderful metaphor for what happens in each of our lives? To my surprise, I found that you can actually practice *shikan taza* in a beach chair. All of my opinions about people sitting in chairs, or half lotus, or *seiza,* dissolved. It was as if a large window opened for me.

When I began to practice Zen in 1960, there was a lot of interest in the martial arts, kendo, and swordsmanship. I remember reading about some techniques in swordsmanship, and in one book it said the best way in combat is to come out, strike your opponent, and quickly get away. In other words, no complicated technique. I thought it sounded like Zen: very simple and direct, and very difficult to do without practice. But the most difficult part for me came where the book confirmed the fact that the combat was to end in a mutual slaying. I didn't like that because I wanted to win. I didn't want to be slain. I wanted to have the gain of winning the contest and ending up alive. But every day within our lives to know how to lose *is* to be alive. Accepting things as they are is a loss. Being in the moment is a loss. We are losing every moment of our lives. What are we losing? We are losing our self-centeredness, our self-clinging, our ideas, our conditioning. We are also losing our selves to the sound of the crickets, to the sound and feeling of the *zendo* as we sit, day after day, night after night. And when we know how to do this, to really lose, then we know how to really be alive.

We generally say that to have a good seat takes ten years. When you think about how long it takes a fruit tree to bloom and bear fruit, ten years is not a very long time. But we shouldn't just understand this literally. Ten years could be *Bam!* striking my stick on the floor, or it could actually be ten years. But generally it does take us some time to cultivate this seat. As I mentioned, Sekito Kisen, the Stone Head Zen master, used to sit on a very large stone. On this stone was carved the Chinese characters that read *genso,* meaning "source of our ancestors." How do you understand this phrase? Of course, Sekito Kisen is our ancestor, but at the same time the ancestor, and the source of the ancestor, is none other than the essence of our own mind source. Do you understand? We are the same as the undying person in the hermitage. That's our source, our most intimate self, appearing in one unbroken moment—preciously, pervasively, quiet, calm, and forever bright.

Do you know what you are doing when you are practicing, when *this* ancestor, your most intimate self, is practicing? You are practicing active participation in loss. We have fear, denial, resistance, sleepiness, exhaustion, and pain. We have the whole spectrum of loss. There's no gain here. Suzuki-roshi used to mention "gaining self." In this kind of situation there's not much gain, because you are participating with loss. That means that even though you are sitting quietly on the cushion, you are actively, energetically participating with the "many things." You are actively participating with pain changing to sensation, with noise changing to sound, with the awareness of distraction or sleepiness, on and on. Because you can practice being with these things, little by little you will not be bothered by these conditions. Awareness vanishes delusion. Even the sound of crickets will harmonize with your mind. When you practice active participation in loss, you are reconditioning yourself to reenter the unconditional world. Actually, this phrase comes from the realized saying by Uchiyama-roshi's teacher, Kodo Sawaki-roshi, who said, "Gain is delusion, loss is enlightenment." In our contemporary language we say, Loss is *where it's at!*

The first noble truth that Buddha realized is that life is suffering. Maybe, like some of you, when I first read this a long time ago, I felt it had a negative connotation. But it's about actively participating with suffering, actively accepting the inevitability of change, which is an undeniable condition of our lives. Things are neither fixed nor permanent but are constantly changing from moment to moment. There is an old saying, "You cannot step into the river in the same place twice." We usually create our own universe. We believe that we can step into the same place twice, because we try to solidify our changing world so that our conditioned self can feel a sense of security. Actually, the whole river is moving, and the entire environment, both river and shore, is changing as well. It's only the fabrication of our minds that we are actually stepping into the same spot twice. But the truth of impermanence is stronger than our mind-fabrications can ever be, and as a result there is plenty of suffering, or loss, that will appear when we ignore this clear fact.

A few years ago we received a wonderful gift at Sonoma Mountain. It was an eleven-faced wooden sculpture of Kannon Bosatsu. She is the mother of all buddhas because of her great mercy and compassion. If you go to the Buddha's birthplace in

Lumbini, Nepal, you will see a temple there built for the Buddha's mother nearly twenty-six hundred years ago. King Ashoka also placed a pillar there, and amazingly it's still standing. I was very impressed with this monument. In our country there are not many buildings built for mothers. When you honor a shrine like this, the best thing to do is to sit *zazen* by turning your light inward. Traditionally when people arrive at a stupa or shrine, the first thing they do is to circumambulate the monument three times by just walking reverently, without thinking, in a sunwise or clockwise direction. Afterward, when you do sit in the way I described, you are returning to loss and silence, which after all are inseparable. Returning there for just a few minutes keeps not only the monument alive but us as well. This is what the monument is all about.

The large Kannon statue we have in our temple was donated by Lee Lozowick, who is the spiritual successor of the East Indian Baul tradition and the Hohm community in Prescott, Arizona. Coincidentally, Maezumi-roshi had done a calligraphy for this statue when it was in their temple. He had written *En mei jukku kannon gyo,* which means "Ten phrase Kannon sutra for prolonging life." When our *sangha* was invited to receive the statue, there was a little dispute. How much would it cost? How big was it? How would we transport it? How much does it weigh? I really didn't have any idea, but when I saw the photo and realized its beauty, I forgot about the details. Then I thought, "Uh-oh, I'm in trouble." Auspiciously, the Hohm community decided to transport it from Prescott to Sonoma Mountain. Lee's daughter, Rami, who was only a few years old, sent a card with the statue. Her father gave it to me. It was in an envelope, and she had scribbled on the card with a yellow crayon. Inside the card was a picture of an umbrella with some rain, and she had signed it with great effort.

There was a drought in the Southwest that year, but as they drove out from Arizona to California, it rained all the way. Kannon arrived on December 7 in the evening. We cleaned and oiled her on the *zendo* deck, with the help of the moonlight. When we stood her up the next morning, it was December 8, Buddha's enlightenment day. Surprisingly, a plaque came with the statue that said it was dedicated in Japan on December 8, 1959. This almost marks the same time Suzuki-roshi came to America. As it turned out, the statue was fourteen feet high, and it now seems as if it has always been standing in our *zendo*.

One of the most distinguishing features of the eleven-faced Kannon is the crown that adorns her head. The main face that you see represents our regular face. Just as when we look in the mirror, it's our face and at the same time it's not our true face. This is very much like Tozan Ryokai's enlightenment poem.* While crossing a stream, he experienced his true reflection in the water, and in that moment he realized that he was not just an object to be seen. On Kannon's crown the first three faces are similar, calm in appearance, and peaceful. As you move sunwise from left to right around the crown, the faces become more and more ghastly, reflecting our agonizing states of suffering, fear, anger, and hopelessness. I find this interesting. It would be difficult for the first three faces on the statue to see the ones on the sides, and even more difficult for them to see the ones in the back, just as it's difficult for us to see or really to face these things within ourselves. But if you wear them as a crown, all the faces become Buddha.

We could say that the fourth face represents anger and hate. With real practice, when you are actively participating in the loss that these conditions demand, your posture, breath, and aware-

---

*Suzuki-roshi's translation of this poem appears on page 236.

ness will gradually dissolve the solidity of these delusional phases because, in the end, they are transparent, and there is nothing behind them. We say, because you are not aware, it's not practiced, and if it's not practiced, it isn't perfected. And if it's not perfected, this fact cannot be realized.

The fifth face expresses anxiety, frustration, and confusion. The sixth, you could say, is isolation and rejection. The seventh, eighth, and ninth represent the most difficult situations we will inevitably face in our lives: devastation, despair, hopelessness. This does not seem to be good news, but because we are fortunate enough to have a Dharma practice, we aren't forced to drink, take drugs, or commit suicide when we meet these faces. Kannon wears all of these faces on her crown; they are a fact of living.

The truth is that as you go around Kannon's crown, you are actually getting closer to something wonderful. Even though your energy may be low and you may not feel well, sometimes in these last phases you look surprisingly good because something is really happening. Finally, you arrive at hopelessness. This is probably the worst one. This is the bottom. But even though there's no more hope, again there's no need to harm yourself, despite your feeling as if there's no ground beneath you and no choice in any direction. The fact that you have no choice can be a good thing because you definitely know which way to go in the midst of this hopelessness. (Actually, the last face to appear is the Buddha, right in the heart of hopelessness.) We know that this is the path, and we resolve to stay with it. In Zen there are no promises made, but we know that this is the practice, too. This is how faith and vow are born in Zen practice. Needless to say, we develop deep faith through our own experience of physical and mental loss.

There is a story that is very relevant when we find ourselves in this condition. One day a monk was walking through the mountain near some cliffs when suddenly she felt the ground slip from beneath her feet. She experienced herself falling, and at the last moment, as she fell, she grabbed on to a branch that was sticking out from the side of the cliff. Frightened, she called out, "Help! Help!" but no one was around to hear her. After some time a teacher and some students who were walking nearby heard her cries and came to the edge of the cliff. When the monk saw them, she shouted, "Please! You've got to help me!" The teacher looked at the situation and said to her, "Just let go!" Isn't that wonderful? "Just let go!" The monk was terrified because she knew she was hanging vertically in midair, high above the ground, and yet here's this teacher telling her to let go. "I can't!" she cried. But the teacher was very firm and clear and told her, "You've got to let go! Without any hesitation, you've got to let go now!" So she did. The monk let go and found that she had not been hanging vertically in midair after all. The entire time she had been lying horizontally on the ground, and the ground had been supporting her all along.

We have so much confusion, so much delusion, our egos have convinced us through our own thoughts that we are hanging vertically and that we're sure to fall straight down into the darkness. But when we do let go, how wonderful. We discover that the darkness is actually full of light. Now we can take a very deep rest, filled with the warmth of relief and complete satisfaction.

When I was in the Southwest recently, the vast landscapes were covered with snow. Although I felt a kind of cold desolation in this environment, I could still see a tip of early spring emerging from within the snow. In southern Colorado I was within the range of the Sangre de Cristo (Blood of Christ) Mountains. The valley there is three times the size of Connecticut, and the mountains are fourteen thousand feet high and very sharp. My feeling was "These are *real* mountains!" Among them was a mountain called Greenhorn, which was rounder and softer than the others, yet it had a very impressive presence. The people I was with told me that this mountain had been under the ocean three times. Isn't that a long time? The sharp and angular ones were the young mountains, and it's perfect that this is so. In the process of active participation in loss, we are worn down by space and time. We are worn down by wind and rain and sun. We are even worn down by the moon and stars. We are just like Greenhorn Mountain. But by actively participating in the wonder of real practice, we realize there is no choice. This realization is a very important one for you to make. Because you *know* this, you will stay on the path; in truth there is no place to go. With the help of Buddha, Dharma, and Sangha, you will go through, through and through, and you will realize what has always been here and what has always been with you. This active participation in loss is our great gift.

I'd like to close with a poem I wrote. I don't write poetry often, but my hope is that I might share with you the precious gift of loss:

> *Night dies into day,*
> *Day dies into night.*
> *Exhaling is intimate with loss,*
> *Inhaling I am renewed.*

18

DIAMOND AND COAL,
THE PURE HEART
OF PRACTICE

Practice is not about experiencing some kind of ecstasy or escape. Practice throws us right into the heart of the fire, right into the situation with the child in the river, because that's where the diamond is formed, under the pressure, in the midst of the heat.

IN THE LATE 1980s, during one of my many summer visits to our *sangha* in Poland, I was invited to visit a coal mine that went to a depth of fifteen hundred feet below sea level. I noticed that all the miners crossed their hearts in front of a statue of the Virgin Mary before they took the fast elevator down. I had never been so far beneath the surface of the earth before, and my imagination went kind of wild. I thought that maybe my watch would blow up, or that there would be an extreme amount of heat or wind in the tunnels or difficult terrain. I told these things to our guide, Alexander, but with a very calm and gentle voice he said, "Well, you know, we're not animals down here."

As you can imagine, working in the mine is very difficult; it shortens your life by perhaps ten years, and usually the miners' faces are accented with black rings of coal dust around their eyes. Besides being difficult, the work is also painstakingly slow. For every two or three feet that you go forward, you have to build walls and a ceiling, and you cannot make a mistake, because your life and the lives of others depend upon doing it correctly. After my day of being in the mine I gained great respect for miners because it's very strenuous and dangerous work. In America we have more machinery available to do this kind of work, but most of the work in Poland is done by hand, and as a result there are a greater number of accidents. I was told that when the Communists were in power, the miners were forced to work seven days a week, which caused some of them to die from accidents or exhaustion.

At one point I couldn't help but ask our guide, "Will we be able to see some coal in this mine?" I felt very much like the baby fish asking the mother fish, as they were swimming in the ocean, "Will we be able to see some water? Where is the water?" Alexander quickly took us over to some pure coal, picked it up, and handed it to me. I was surprised: Pure coal is not the coal that we are used to. It's very shiny, and no black dust rubs off when you touch it, so it cannot dirty your hands. I also picked up some chunky pieces of pure coal, and when my hands didn't become dirty, I really came to appreciate this as a metaphor. It's a fact that if pure coal remains in the ground under a lot of pressure for a great length of time, it transforms into a clear diamond. Black, chunky coal turns into translucent, very hard diamond. It is almost the hardest thing in the world.

When you come to practice or study Zen, you have to exhaust your energy, you have to throw your life-force into your practice, whatever you're doing. It's like being a kind of miner. This is very important. It may be difficult for many of us to do this because we have so many hindrances, so many fears and inhibitions that keep us separated from life—both the life within ourselves and the life in what we usually call "outside." We are always separated from our lives into what we call the subject and the object. But no matter what situation you find yourself in, everything you encounter in your life is practice, is the Self, and when you throw yourself entirely into what you are doing, that's Zen. To be able to realize this, and to fully do it, it may not even matter whether you have training or not, though hopefully the training you receive at our Zen Center and others will help. But sometimes we understand our training in such a way that we just end up becoming professional Zen people, experts in Zen. When this is the case, it doesn't help, because that's not the point of training.

As I've mentioned before, the first teacher you will meet at a Zen center is the schedule. No matter what you may want to do or not do, the schedule provides a kind of natural pressure that pushes you past your hindrances, past your ideas of yourself and your fears or inhibitions. It pushes you to do things you may not like: stopping work at a certain time, going to meetings, eating food that may not have the taste you particularly enjoy, going to sleep early so you can wake up *very* early, sitting long hours. All of this pressure begins to accumulate like frost gathering on snow; it functions like the pressure that transforms coal into diamond.

In California during the 1960s many people expressed the feeling that "returning to nature" was the way to live: watching the sun set over the ocean, or maybe having the easy life of sitting in a beach chair all day long. People felt that sitting at the beach or doing only what you liked and being laid back was okay. But that may not be a real understanding of "returning to nature." If you watch something natural like the small birds that fly outside our *zendo,* birds about the size of finches with very long beaks, you will see that they follow a very natural pattern. If you observe them carefully, you'll see that they always go spiraling sunwise up the redwood's giant trunk in a particular way. *That's* nature. If there is a rock in a pond, the fish who live there will swim around it and become large and strong. If there is no rock, the fish will remain small. That's nature, too. And nature is also how coal becomes diamond.

The heart of the bird and the fish is pure. Most people understand that. But our hearts are also pure. Hui Neng, our Sixth Ancestor, said that originally not one weed is found inside ourselves. So we don't have to try to be good or natural because we already are, only we don't know it. We don't have to try to be more than ourselves, more than we think we are when we look at ourselves with that judgmental, discriminating mind that separates us from life, because our hearts are already pure. This is our "nature," and we should take care to remind each other of this in our practice.

It would be fair to say that in Poland I was under a lot of pressure. One of our Polish *sangha* members described it wonderfully when he said that there were two hundred *dokusan* in three weeks. But that wasn't quite true. Usually *dokusan* is an intimate meeting with *roshi* held in the *dokusan* room. But I really have to laugh because *everywhere* I went was a *dokusan.* If I had breakfast, I didn't have breakfast by myself or with one other person, but instead there would be eight, ten, or twelve people there with me, and they would be very anxious to ask some kind of question, either about the practice or about themselves or about their personal life. Life is very intense in Poland, and the people are very good people. Because I visit only once a year, the need is very intense and strong.

At the annual *sesshin* there was a young girl attending named Malgosia, who is only nine years old. She had attended the seven-day *sesshin* with the adults the year before, and she asked permission to come again. Her schedule is modified, but she participates and she's engaged. For *dokusan* she comes in and asks a question just like everyone else. Last year she asked me, "Roshi, how old are you?" It's really wonderful how she steps forward. I answered, "As old as you think," with a smile.

When I was in Germany, I had the chance to spend some time with a father and his two children, one of them a five-year-old girl. I had some candy with me, so I gave some to her and her brother. When I did, I noticed that they were extremely shy children, looking down at the ground, almost as if they had no hands. Her father had brought me a card that she had written in German—a five-year-old girl! The card said, "The whole world is beautiful!" With an exclamation point. That's really wonderful.

As adults we often become more and more tainted. We lose the purity of heart that this little girl expressed because our own ignorance allows us to accept the separation from life as if this condition is true. But we should know that the separation is what causes greed, anger, and ignorance to flourish. Because we don't really know this, we entertain that separation to our own detriment and the detriment of our loved ones and the world around us. So I encourage you to become truly engaged in your practice; then you will be able to be aware of how this process occurs.

I don't know if Zen will ever become popular. Usually people want a religion that gives them some kind of promise: If you do this, then you will get that. Most people want this kind of confirmation. We want some great reward at the end of our lives because we've been such good people. But Zen is different. As Hui Neng said, we already are good people. Again, not one weed is found inside us. We don't have to *be* good people, or *become* good people, since we already *are* good people. Zen doesn't promise anything. There's no heaven at the end if you act in a certain way. Even with regard to enlightenment, as it says in Dogen's Genjo Koan, "some may and some may not." The Zen approach is less comforting for many people, but I think it is much more real.

As all of you know, in each and every country in the world people have experienced a tremendous amount of suffering and pain: the Native Americans in this country, the Tibetans in Tibet and China, the people in Iceland who have only recently received their fishing rights from Scandinavia, the people in North and South Korea who lost entire families and whose lineage ended after the division at the thirty-eighth parallel in the early 1950s. Try to imagine it all. Imagine yourself in Berlin after the wall had been constructed. Sometimes a child would fall into the river that flowed there. People on both sides would watch the child struggling in the water, and at the same time they would watch each other with fear. Should you jump in to save the child and take a chance of being shot? People actually saw this happen. What would you do? How would you deal with that degree of pain and suffering? How would you live with the nightmares after seeing such a thing? How would you justify your action in your everyday life?

All over the world we see that people are becoming tired of being misused and abused. This is a good sign, I think, because it means that people are getting fed up with their unjust situation. In our sitting practice we create a space for things to emerge that we ordinarily tend to bury deeply in our minds. It is so important to have this "zone" where we can look at and acknowledge these things so that they can pass through.

When I began to practice, I didn't give much thought to the practice and what it would do or what it would address. When I look back on it, I actually used practice as a kind of escape or refuge where I would not have to deal with anything, just the opposite of what I should have been doing. To tell the truth, I did that for many years. But in real practice these hidden things emerge, and when they do, you are ready to receive them and let them go their own way without delving into their psychology or analyzing them at all. In fact, in practice this is exactly what we work on. Practice is not about experiencing some kind of ecstasy or escape. Practice throws us right into the heart of the fire, right into the situation with the child in the river, because that's where the diamond is formed, under the pressure, in the midst of the heat.

Those who practice Rinzai Zen engage in koan study and have to see their teacher a few times in one day to answer questions that appear just impossible to answer. But having to practice in a way that eventually makes it possible for you to answer these impossible questions yourself trains you to answer them in your everyday life. For a long time I assumed there was more pressure in that school than in our school, but actually there's equal pressure all over. In living life no one is off the hook. One school doesn't exclusively have the most pressure. It's how we understand and use that pressure, what it does to us, that transforms us into diamonds.

In our practice we work hard. In the afternoon, when everyone else is working and you start thinking, "Maybe I'll just take a short nap," you don't do it. A Bodhisattva's path is that you don't save time. This is very different from being burned out at a job, because your faith and purpose are quite different. Throwing yourself into the work burns up your karma. It also burns up greed, anger, and ignorance as well as the past, future, and even the present. That's why you actually *throw* yourself into sitting practice, even when you're tired, because the pressure is good. If you have no pressure, you have no diamond, just black dusty coal.

Do you understand what I mean by pressure? There's a certain pace with which you live your life, and there's a certain kind of faith and belief system you have for your life that is not based on greed, anger, and ignorance. In fact, we put our trust in the Buddha, Dharma, and Sangha. Not so much the historical Buddha but the awakened part of ourselves, the diamond within us and the inevitable possibility of that diamond surfacing.

The nature of Zen practice is very difficult, but so is human nature. We need something strong to match it. We need some kind of training, not just of the thinking mind but of the body as well, because they are one whole. It really isn't enough for us to just wish we were good people, or to try to think ourselves into being good people, because our body and mind may be practicing something else. So it just won't work. We actually have to train the body and train the mind. Our way is to train them with the breath. The breath is the bridge between body and mind, and we entrust our existence to our breath and our sitting posture.

In Poland, after the miners take out the coal, they usually fill the walls of the tunnels with sand to keep them from caving in. But now they are filling them with toxic materials and nuclear waste because they need the money, so the owners of the mines are being paid to store this waste from Germany and the

Netherlands. And this toxic waste is directly beneath their cities. When we do something in one place and then move on, we may think that what we have done won't bother us "over here," where we are now. But over there *is* over here. This is a basic understanding that comes both from the Buddhadharma and from deep ecology. Even when something is done thousands of miles away, it can affect us over here. Whatever we do affects others and the environment across the world. I'm not referring solely to the creation of pollution outside of ourselves, because there is quite a bit of pollution inside ourselves as well. Our thinking mind can produce quite a bit of gossip and abusive garbage that go on and on and on.

It is for this reason that our practice and training are so important for ourselves, for others and the world around us. The practice wears out the internal gossip and garbage and allows the pure coal that does not dirty the hands to emerge. Under pressure wonderful things happen, wonderful things that must happen, because our lives are not really just our own. We must try to see how we are interconnected and that we can respond to and on behalf of one another as part of our practice. The best way to do this is to make the effort to see what you're doing yourself. Try it out as you go through your day. Practice this kind of awareness by asking yourself, "What am I doing?" This will help you to join those who are practicing to decrease the amount of pain and suffering in their lives and in the world at large. And this will put you under some kind of natural pressure. The pressure is similar to when I strike my stick against the floor, *Bam!* or smack my hands together in midair. It does that with our life. I invite you to come to Sonoma Mountain for some pressure. Please join us and find out what Zen is. You can find out. Of course, we're not finding out about Zen, some Asian philosophy, we're finding out about *this* Zen, *this* person. We're not just studying Buddhism, we're investigating who this self really is. It's easier when you practice with people because everyone else is doing it, too. Everybody will encounter some difficulty; even a baby has difficulty. But at the same time just like that little girl wrote on a three-by-four-inch piece of paper: "The whole world is beautiful!" She had the courage and insight and clarity to really know that and to write it down. And so do we.

19

You Can't Get Off the Train

Working with the practice called the compassion breath, you know how to transmute what you see, hear, smell, taste, touch, and think every day. And the truth is that, with practice, this process helps you learn to be kind to yourself and to all beings as well.

WHENEVER I GIVE A TALK, the listeners and I may find ourselves in a paradoxical situation: As words and phrases can often become abstractions, I try to explain something that can't be explained, and the listeners try to hear something that can't be heard. Since by necessity this is the situation, we can sympathize with each other; me with you for that which you can't hear, and you with me for that which I can't say. At the same time I can always strike my stick on the floor, *Bam!* so at least this is possible. Maybe I can't explain it, but I can demonstrate it, and then the rest is up to you.

This can cause a certain amount of frustration on your side and loneliness on mine. But the bigger question is, How can we come together? And how can we realize ourselves? When we chant words like "for all sentient beings," it's pretty abstract. But it becomes less abstract when we begin to find out what *this* sentient being is, and that includes discovering what things go into making up this sentient being. All of our dualistic thoughts and deluded feelings, whether they're good or bad, whether we like them or not, are a sentient being. Our meditation practice is not about trying to deny these aspects of ourselves. Many people have this misunderstanding, but the truth is quite the opposite.

In Poland I met with a woman who is in her early sixties. Since the end of World War II all of her memories of the war have been suppressed. For some reason, however, at this time of her life all of her memories are returning and surfacing. What is she to do with them? What are any of us to do with the content of our mind? How can each of us work with our own situation? This is the practice of meditation.

Each one of us holds the very same wish and aspiration: to be able to work with the difficulties that life brings us, based on the awareness we cultivate through our practice. As you continue your journey and your practice grows, you will see that there's a beginning and a middle and an end that, in reality, are all the same. For convenience, or because we are speaking about it, we separate this One, this Same, into three parts, but actually it is just One. In time you will discover this for yourselves, unless you become scared and run off—which, believe it or not, happens frequently. But what comes up in our meditation is not new. It's old stuff, and you can only run off so many times before you realize that there's no need to run anymore. For many people that's the moment when their practice begins to engage.

The late Uchiyama-roshi explained that there is a seed or cause that has auspiciously brought you in contact with the path. This alone points you in the direction of Dharma. This is one interpretation of Dharma: looking for something that seems to be missing. Maybe some truth is what is lacking in life, and at a certain point we are actually able to experience this. Either through our grief, or our experience of sickness, loss, or a change in relationship, or just a feeling of impermanence that is no longer tolerable, we begin to look and to quest, and we begin to practice *zazen* as part of that quest.

What *zazen* really is has been explained in many different ways. Suzuki-roshi used to say *shikan taza* is our *zazen,* but as I've mentioned, the words and phrases used to express Zen practice can sound pretty abstract, and almost any explanation is conceptual. It can't really touch the experience itself. Suzuki-roshi put it very simply: "Just to be ourselves." Four words, but what they express is so deep and so subtle that we miss it until we begin slowing down. He said our practice is following our breath. But the true meaning of this, the deep meaning, is that you are vividly *alive.* The method says to follow your breath, but its meaning is that you are invisibly present and alive, just like a spinning top that goes faster and faster until it disappears. Without method, without expectation, without counting your breath, you are alive moment to moment; alive in this space that is nowhere else but right here within yourself. Others have said that *zazen* or *shikan taza* means being present in this very moment, but even that's not it. It's *being* the moment. It's being each moment after moment after moment in *zazen,* before *zazen,* and after *zazen* as well. And of course that's the manifestation or actualization of your original mind. "Just to be ourselves." This is *shikan taza.*

Every year when I travel to meet with students in Poland, the schedule is very intense. Last year when I was standing beside a window on a hot and crowded train going from Gdansk to Warsaw, just watching the scenery go by, suddenly I became acutely aware that my breath had become naturally deeper than it had been before. After some time I became aware of the sound of my breath and began to follow it. It was very wonderful because I was unaware that more than three hours passed by. I felt only that I was being embraced by the sound's traveling.

You pass a lot of scenery when you're on a train. In Poland we passed devastated environments, broken-down homes, and the families who live there watching trains while standing or working outside, lots of garbage and litter everywhere (I did see some good graffiti, too!), and also beautiful forests and plains. I was receiving all of this as it passed by, and at the same time I was aware of my breath. Even though I had been standing the entire time, after the train reached its destination I got off and felt completely renewed.

When you practice like this, you receive everything you see on the inhalation of the breath. You don't pretend not to see it. In our contemporary lives we pretend a lot in order to protect ourselves. There's TV, newspapers with bad news, city noises, and so many other things that seem to be assaulting us. But no matter what it is, you can take it in, and because you do receive it, on the exhalation you can let it out. You let it go. This is the *shikan taza* breath. It can be compared to the alchemy of turning lead into gold. You fill up with your sorrow or anger or any other feeling that you usually try to avoid, and by doing so you acknowledge that it is there. But this is only part of the practice, because the fact that you have done it means that, on the exhale, you release it and let it go. It actually needs this acknowledgment in order to be really released.

It's a little odd, but in general we tend not to be aware of other people's anger, or even our own anger, despite the fact that our whole meditation practice is about awareness. What you *can* do, what you *can't* do, what you want or don't want to do, is still about awareness. Our practice is to have the courage to actually feel and accept these aspects of being human. They're just a small part of us, and our practice will help us to make room so that we can receive and feel these things and therefore let them go without attaching to them, just as you receive and release the passing scenery when you're on a train.

I think it's pretty true to say that we're all on a train. The scenery is going by quickly, and you can't hold on to anything; you have to stay and keep going down the track. It's when you hold on to something, or even try to hold on, that you are not on the train anymore. But our way tells us to release what we are holding so that we can keep going and stay on track. What it really comes down to is the wisdom and compassion of non-avoidance. You just keep going, and as you do, working with the practice called the *compassion breath,* you know how to transmute what you see, hear, smell, taste, touch, and think every day. And the truth is that, with practice, this process helps you learn to be kind to yourself and to all beings as well.

We have the capacity to take in an enormous amount of negativity and to let it go its way. We don't avoid anything because we know we can work with it. Most people don't know what to do when they notice unwanted thoughts and feelings within themselves, or see a dead animal on the road, or killing on television shows or in the news, or the many homeless and starving people right beside them as they walk down the street. And then there's drugs, alcohol, AIDS, and cancer. People feel overwhelmed, and the result is that often their hearts turn hard and cold. I'm sorry to say it, but it's true. The normal response to these things would be that everyone should be crying—this is the awakening of compassion—but the ignorance of sentient beings causes us to continue to enhance samsara. The practice of *compassion breath* allows our hearts to remain soft and open while our spirit and life-force are replenished. And our tears are part of this replenishment, an important part. You do not have to be a Buddhist to do this; it is meant to be used by all human beings, everywhere, even while standing on a train.

The Tibetan Buddhist nun Ani Tenzin Palmo said that compassion practice is a form of discipline. Most people really don't like discipline, but it's necessary. Maybe it would be easier to say it's preparation, but whatever word we use, we need discipline and preparation for the effort to stay on the train and allow the scenery to go by. Pretty soon, even before you know it, you'll be sixty, and that's not so old. Scenery changes quickly.

When you're a child, a day seems to last a long time. Sometimes at the grocery store in town you may see a father holding a baby, and the baby is completely surrendered into the father's arms. The child's body/mind shows its purity and trust. As the child becomes older, naturally it wants to grow in all ways. Then in almost no time at all summer holidays don't come so often, the seasons drift by, new babies are born, and at a certain age friends start dying. This is true for every one of us. But regardless of what age we are, we should do our best to see the whole picture.

When we talk about "saving all sentient beings," we are talking about everyone in that picture and also all forms of life. But the real meaning of the phrase remains beyond our reach and again is pretty abstract. Our practice can help you to make a good start toward breaking down that abstraction by revealing how you can take in and release your suffering, which includes the suffering of others. It's not uncommon at the beginning of this practice for people to feel a little afraid to allow suffering to come in. If this is true in your case, you can practice imagining yourself doing it, or pretending, until you see what's actually there. The point is that as you begin to do this, little by little you are actually transforming what you receive. And little by little from the particular you make your way into universal suffering by imagining all the other people in the world with the same feelings and conditions you have who are suffering exactly like you. Now your suffering is in the right perspective, and it's no longer personal.

Compassion practice includes your active participation in accepting this suffering, but that is not all. At the same time that you take all of this in and then release it, there still is the blue sky and the bright morning sun shining on the green grass, though even a dark sky will do. And you begin to realize that confusion and suffering are also void, empty, and nonsubstantial.

Do you understand? You're on a train, and the scenery is going by. Included in the scenery are all the ways in which you project upon yourself, abuse yourself, or create a dialogue within yourself that occupies a whole day, or three days, or maybe a week, and still you aren't aware of it. Then at the end of the day you're so tired, completely exhausted, but still you're on the train, holding on, and the tighter you hold on to the passing scenery, the more the train seems to drag to a stop. In reality the train doesn't stop, it continues on, living dying living dying, but in our deluded understanding we've stopped the train. We've even gotten off the train! The fabrication or delusional system of our small minds is that powerful. We believe we've stopped the whole train and gotten off, and maybe we've even stayed for a couple of days or months. Some people pass their entire lives this way. But the train is going on. Believe it or not, it continues on. And while it does, while this whole drama flies through space and time, you can actually apply your compassion practice to engage your suffering and the suffering you see in the world around you, and experience how to let the grip go. Even doing this much begins to transform all that lead into gold.

In the late 1970s the Tibetan teacher Chögyam Trungpa Rinpoche introduced to his community certain practices for difficult times. He was one of the most controversial and influential Tibetan teachers to transmit Dharma to the West, and he and Suzuki-roshi had a very close relationship that our traditions continue to this day. There's really nothing anywhere like the practices he introduced, which include compassionate breathing. We're so fortunate to have some kind of practice that can work with the unwanted thoughts and feelings that cause suffering and fear.

When Rinpoche first said, "Let's try to take on the suffering of other people," he was quite shocked at the response. Most of the students said they didn't want to do it. Suzuki-roshi wanted to encourage us in the same direction, but he was more subtle and mild, and so he would say the same thing but in a gentle way. He would say that "the Bodhisattva path" or "to help other people" is our Way. But the truth is that most of us were not really on the Mahayana path; we were just interested in our own self-realization. Suzuki-roshi knew this, and I think that's why he presented it in the way he did. And it did help us, because we do have to realize which track we are on.

It is said that having the capacity, the foundation, and the vessel to take on the suffering of others is one of the great joys, because you can make someone else happy, not just yourself. Of course, we usually do not realize, as we do this for someone, that

that other person's joy includes our joy, too. But when you focus just on yourself, your universe becomes smaller and smaller. Eventually it becomes as tiny as the head of a pin. That's it. There's no spaciousness. There's no room for joy. There's no humor. There's no curiosity. There's no discovery. In this way your world becomes so diminished that you have imprisoned yourself within your own conditioned mind.

There are more than six billion other people in the world at this time, and many of them look exactly like you. It's true. They have a character and karmic pattern just like you. I see students from around the world quite a bit, and I can see an American, a Pole, an Icelander, a Chinese, and for each country there is an equal. When I was in Iceland recently, I saw someone walking down the street, and I said, "Oh, there's Gary! In Iceland!" You really do wonder sometimes when you see the same karmic force, the same values and ideas, the same features, build, and color, as someone on the other side of the world.

Think of all the people who have the same feeling you have—maybe of failure or of anger at someone. Sometimes when we become very angry, we can do something about it in the situation, and sometimes we can't. So who do you beat up? Guess. You know the answer; the closest one to you is yourself. And you do it even though you may not be aware that you are doing it. This is why we have to become softer. We just need to be kinder to ourselves because we deserve it. Why beat ourselves up? Isn't it better to just let go of the dialogue? Let it go completely? We've been doing this for thirty, forty, fifty years. It's very strong conditioning. And our compassion is the practice of *uncondi-tioning*. We already have the discipline, and we already have the strength, so all we have to do is to let it go. Little by little allow the old story line to dissolve.

But it isn't so easy. Even when we decide to take on the practice of acknowledging and letting go, we may fear that if we do let go, something terrible may happen to us. Probably something even worse. You may be in the present, but it can be quite frightening to be in the present. Let me assure you that being in the present won't hit you like the first time you smoked marijuana or had some LSD or peyote or whatever new "designer drug" people are taking these days. It won't overwhelm you like that because it's organic. It comes from within.

When Hoitsu Suzuki-roshi went out for a smoke one day, Sojun Weitsman's little boy asked him, "Roshi, what are you doing?" This is the ultimate Zen question you have to ask yourselves, "What are you doing? What's going on?" If you do this, you will begin to not accept habit or impulse as your way of life.

When you are practicing, please remember that your breathing is very important. Even those of us who sit every day may forget to apply it, but do your best to remember the breathing. On the inhalation you take in some of the suffering—either your own or someone else's—and on the exhalation you let it go. Repeat this three or four times, receiving and releasing, taking in and letting go. Then you may move from the personal to the universal. That's it. Even if you're not practicing this on an intense schedule, if you just practice it for a minute or two or three when you're sitting or standing in your ordinary life, you will have some experience you can begin to rely on. This is true even when you're doing it for someone who's quite far away from you or who is dead. Try it. Do it for someone who is alive, someone you do not like, or someone who is dying. It will also clean up your own negativity, your own karma. This *compassion breath* will burn it up.

As I have mentioned, once I painted a traditional Zen circle made in just one stroke, known in Japanese as an *enso,* and wrote, "Breath sweeps mind." Just the sound of the breath painted it. We can hardly hear our breath because we are so busy listening to our thinking all the time. Twenty-four hours a day, just the same. Are we that conditioned that we don't get tired of it? You may say yes, but maybe you aren't tired enough. You say you are, but I'm not convinced, because when you really are tired enough, you will change. Your behavior will begin to change, and you will take up this practice wholeheartedly. Life isn't that long, and besides no one else can do it for you. You're the only one who can turn your lead, your heavy stuff, into gold. That's all you have to do, and you can do it through the breath. That's what we practice in the *zendo,* and that's what you can practice outside, in the bigger *zendo,* in action.

His Holiness the Dalai Lama has said many times that it is not the Buddhist way to just accept something on faith. We should put everything to the test and decide for ourselves whether to have faith in it. So there is a relationship between action and faith in the Buddhadharma. That's why I encourage you to put this practice to the test. You can start by taking a look and seeing for yourself where you spend most of your life. In bed? On your feet? On your seat? And while you're there, what is it that you are doing? What do you long for? Everything to change? Nothing to change?

Somewhere deep within most of us we're not convinced that we can really make a shift or change. When we hear a teaching such as this, something inside of us is conditioned to reject it and say it's just another fantasy we shouldn't take seriously. So I don't know what it takes. Our conditioning is so strong that maybe the rug has to be pulled from beneath our feet, or the whole floor has to drop away. Believe me, I know from my own experience.

BREATH OR KEEPS MIND

SONOMA

Even when I was in the hospital, after a cancer operation, I was still smoking. Can you believe it? That's how stupid we are! I had a carton of cigarettes in my lower drawer. That's how much I was in denial and unaware of addiction. But whatever we practice is what we get. It's really true. So if you're practicing abusing yourself, all I can say is that it's not beneficial to yourself or others.

That's why I want to encourage you to try. Even though your delusion practice is excellent and maintains its energy, exhausting and undermining you at the end of the day, and you get carried away with it every time, you should still try. At least during meditation practice, when it comes up, you can be aware of it. And gradually in your world, in the big *zendo* in action, you can become aware of it. You have some way to work with your conditioning, your life, and your world; some real way that is not abstract but solid, to help you to stay on the train.

20

THE RIVER LONGS
TO RETURN
TO THE OCEAN

*We should go from the outer form of Zen to the inner form
of Zen; the inherent form inside us, which we have always
had and which is our own treasure.*

WHEN I WAS in Poland I said to the *sangha,* "The
river longs to return to the ocean." As I've thought
more about it, I've realized that this phrase
expresses a theme that seems to run throughout our lives. We are
all rivers here in this world who long to return to the ocean. It is
one of the main reasons people meditate, to help us return to our
treasure. But the fact that you think you meditate doesn't mean
that you *are* meditating and that all of your problems will be
solved. In one of Thich Nhat Hanh's more humorous stories, he
tells about a Korean woman whose practice was daily chanting.
(There's a strong chanting tradition in Korea. Zen master Seung
Sahn was enlightened while chanting. One of the chanting practices is called *kido,* which can be translated as "energy path." It
involves very repetitive and intensive chanting while striking per-

cussion instruments and walking in a particular pattern or form for many hours a day. No sitting, just chanting. Because of the intensity of practice, you can actually return to the sourceless source of the sound.)

According to Thich Nhat Hanh, this woman named Mrs. Lee practiced chanting every day for ten years. But her neighbors knew that she was still an angry person; she wasn't very nice or kind. One day Mrs. Lee was practicing in her little apartment and striking her *moktak*, which is a hollow wooden percussive instrument held in the hand and sounded with a striker to help people maintain the rhythm of the chant. While she was chanting, her neighbor took the trouble to come to her house to deliver an important message. Because she was chanting and striking the *moktak*, she didn't hear him at the door, so he stood outside and called up to her, "Mrs. Lee!" She thought she heard something, but she kept on chanting. After a while she realized that her neighbor was calling her: "Mrs. Lee! Mrs. Lee!" But she kept on chanting and calling the names of the Buddha, all the time becoming more and more furious at this neighbor for imposing his voice over her sacred chanting. Finally, she was so angry she threw her *moktak* down on the floor, came to the window, and shouted, "What do you want? Can't you see that I'm a holy person, that I'm practicing and calling the Buddha's name?" He said, "Geez, Mrs. Lee, I only called your name about twelve times. You must have called the Buddha's name at least a million times over the last ten years. He must be *really* furious by now."

A few years ago my older sister Alice sent me a newspaper photograph of some Korean monks fighting in Seoul. In the photo the street was filled with more than a hundred fighting monks. One of them had a long board and was just about to hit another monk. They were fighting over a very ancient and venerated temple, Chogye Sah, that stood near the headquarters. Traditionally, many people came from Seoul and South Korea just to feel the peaceful vibrations of this ancient temple, the power of the place, so whichever group of monks won the fight would have control of the temple. When my sister sent me the photo, it was pretty disturbing. After considering the photo and the situation for some time, I mustered up enough courage to send Zen master Seung Sahn a poem. In the first line, the Korean word *Aieeego* means "very sad."

> *"AIEEEGO! AIEEEGO!"*
> *Monks fighting.*
> *Have they not heard:*
> *Mountains stand tall and*
> *Rivers run long?*

He sent me back a letter that said, "Well, it's just that monks are young; they'll grow up and understand what's happening."

What I'm trying to say is that we are sitting here on this mountain, but are we really sitting just *like* the mountain? Are we sitting with the same lack of understanding as the Korean monks, or Mrs. Lee, or are we really practicing *zazen*?

People like to do *zazen,* that's their main focus, but they don't know that in everyday life everything is *zazen*. Someone said that wanting to do *zazen* but ignoring the schedule is like trying to grow peas without the pod. You're interested in the peas, but the peas come with the pod. It's the pod that protects the pea. In a Zen community the pod is the rhythm of the schedule.

Recently when we were visited by a class of Sonoma State

University students, I was trying to explain what *schedule* means. When we think of the word *schedule,* it's kind of distasteful. People don't really like this word. But as we and the students were doing *qi gong* in the field near the Zen hall as part of our morning schedule, we noticed that twenty-two wild turkeys showed up at the same time every day. "That's schedule," I told them. The male turkeys had stunning masked faces: pure white and bright blue with red beaks and throats, not to mention the exquisite arrangement of brilliant feathers worn almost like the ceremonial costume of a samurai. The turkeys are smarter than you think. With all that weight, they could still quickly fly—fast and safe. And they know where to go at a certain time in a twenty-four-hour day. There's a place that's a reference point for them, and they go there naturally.

Each of us should know in our life: Where do we go? What is our reference point? Because they know this, the turkeys remain alive. But how do we remain alive? Whether it's outside or inside, there's someplace we should go. Inside is the most important place. You should go somewhere, and you should know where that place is and how to get there. It's the same for all beings, whether they are animals or humans. Since Sonoma is a wild mountain and the possibilities are infinite here, the turkeys go to a certain place because they know instinctively that they will die if they don't. What if every day they took a new route? "Let's go this way today, we went that way yesterday." In a pretty short amount of time their lives may end. For them and for us, it's "Go down this one-way street, take this alley, walk down this way, over here, and then back."

So many of us fear repetition. We live in a society that always demands that things be *new, new, new* and *fast, fast, fast.* But what is this newness bringing us? It doesn't seem that things are getting better even with all this new technology. Most people have not discovered a way to know their true nature or to become intimate with their original mind. What these terms express is completely foreign to them. So I don't think our focus on what is new and fast can ever deeply satisfy us in this way. It's the repetition, the power of repetition, the very opposite of distraction, that helps to calm and soothe the mind and heart. This is what gives us the sense that there is some place that is a refuge, a place that holds the assurance that we know we are here, that we can in all ways return to this space, and that we know how to arrive. We are going home. Like the river we are returning to the ocean. That's where we really want to go.

Hannyatara Dai Osho, who was Bodhidharma's teacher, wrote something very important, very simple and wonderful. It points to the clarity, and the way, of our practice:

> *When I inhale,*
> *I don't dwell upon things.*
> *When I exhale,*
> *I don't pursue thoughts.*
> *Thus I breathe the sutra,*
> *As-it-is-ness.*
> *Hundreds of thousands of millions of times.*

This is exquisite. This is the pinnacle of Zen: seeing *things as it is.* Though it is not always so, little by little, through long training and long practice, through your *zazen,* you will realize that your original mind, where the river no longer longs but *is* ocean, is just like this. I hope you will embrace this as your own experience, your own intimacy, and not just listen to it as something coming from someone else. "When I inhale, I don't dwell on things." You're free, free of thoughts, and so much alive, vividly, joyously alive within this very life. It's so spacious, calm, clear, and bright.

Of course, in the beginning of your practice it may be more like "I'm not thinking!" and then all the thoughts pour in. That's okay. That's just how it is. But after experiencing this a hundred thousand million times, you learn how to work with your mind, and you begin to experience this truth: "When I exhale, I don't pursue thoughts." This is the same as my early motto, "Breath sweeps mind." It doesn't mean you lose your ability to think, it means that you don't pursue the thoughts because you are returning to the ocean. And when you repeat this a hundred thousand million times, you will be intimate with the great ease and great perfection of *zazen*.

The first time I heard the phrase *menmitsu no kafu* I was in my early thirties, very young and eager. I heard it in a talk given by Tatsugami-roshi, who was the *ino* from Eihei-ji Monastery, but actually it comes from the Chinese Zen master Seigen Gyoshi. It expresses his way of being very careful, very considerate and aware. What impressed me so deeply was that when Tatsugami-roshi gave the talk, he didn't move one inch. He just remained still and looked down at the floor and spoke in an even voice flowing from some oceanic place. He mentioned *menmitsu no kafu,* and at the time I thought it simply meant we had to be very careful with everything we did. When you put something down, you do it carefully. When you put your shoes together, you do it carefully. But that's just the shell around the peas, the outer form. We should go from the outer form of Zen to the inner form of Zen; the inherent form inside us, which we have always had and which is our own treasure. When you glimpse that inner form, you know why you put your shoes together, what *menmitsu no kafu* really means. On one occasion you may throw a book down, and that's okay, but oftentimes you lay it down. The point is that you do both with the same spirit.

Whether you throw something or lay it down, when you do it with the spirit that recognizes its liveliness, the inherent quality or virtue of the object, animate or inanimate, you simultaneously recognize this within yourself. Everything is complete in your form. We are not talking about something outside ourselves. This is the basic Dharma, the basic teaching. Don't forget. Don't forget what you have or what you are. The river longs to return to what it already is. Don't forget. Don't forget. And please help me to remember, too. We remember together. That's how it is.

21

FINDING OURSELVES
JUST AS WE ARE

*Through practice, when the deluded mind dissolves into
darkness, another presence emerges that I have referred to
as returning to calm and quiet, like an Icelandic landscape
of infinite beauty, spaciousness, and peace. That's where
zazen mind, or the universal mind that we all intimately
share, is so great and vast, without beginning or end.*

URING THE COMINGS AND GOINGS of seasons
on Sonoma Mountain we have had many teachers visit
us. It's a real gift to spend even a little time with each
of them because they have been practicing for a very long time.
You can see and feel the expansiveness, the lightness, and the joy
that staying with the Dharma may bring to our lives. But not all
of them have been Zen masters. For example, Mitsu Suzuki-
sensei, Suzuki-roshi's wife, has studied and taught tea ceremony
for many years, and you can feel these qualities in her through
and through. We need to realize that we are not just who we
think we are. Nor are other people who we think they are. True
nature is beyond our wildest imagination. We should know by
now that our conditioned, thinking mind can operate only in the

light, and that's where it ends. Through practice, when the deluded mind dissolves into darkness, another presence emerges that I have referred to as returning to calm and quiet, like an Icelandic landscape of infinite beauty, spaciousness, and peace. That's where *zazen* mind, or the universal mind that we all intimately share, is so great and vast, without beginning or end.

You cannot know this universal mind, this Big Mind, only by thinking about it, just as you can't just think yourself into being a good person. Body and mind require discipline. Because our dualistic thinking is so strong, we must return our body and mind to its original oneness. That's why in our practice the body goes through a tremendous amount of discipline and training. We're almost like spiritual athletes, taking delusion's energy and using it—exhausting it—in our *zazen,* chanting, bowing, work practice, all of our temple life. This in turn burns up our greed, anger, and ignorance and turns them into nutritious food.

In the Japanese Zen tradition practitioners really move each other around physically; it's part of their training. But when we move each other around here in America, people often feel insulted. We have to be open enough to move each other around when there's a posture that needs help. And we should allow others to support us and our practice so that we may correct the disharmony. What are we holding on to so tightly?

In the introduction to her book of haiku poems, *Temple Dusk,* Mrs. Suzuki talks about her relationship with Suzuki-roshi. When she visited us here, she said that Suzuki-roshi was not a very good husband but was a very good teacher. I remember the day very well when Mrs. Suzuki first came to San Francisco in 1961 or 1962 because for us it was more than exciting. We all went to the pier to welcome her. The ship on which she traveled from Japan was not exactly a luxury liner. In those days people came over on tankers and cargo ships. As the ship approached, we saw a tiny figure on board who was waving vigorously, wholeheartedly. It was not a weak kind of waving at all. Of course, the figure became larger and larger, and this was Mrs. Mitsu Suzuki.

When they had breakfast together, Suzuki-roshi, being a traditional Zen master from Japan, would eat very quickly: just eating. No conversation. When he finished the meal, he would stand, roll up his sleeves, and go to work because it was time for *samu*. That was his training and background. One day Mrs. Suzuki asked, "Why don't you stick around a little bit and talk to me?" He said, "It's time for *samu*."

Mrs. Suzuki knew that he didn't intend anything mean by acting like this, and actually Mrs. Suzuki is kind of a rascal in her own special way. One time she told Suzuki-roshi, "I have a boyfriend." And he said, "You do? Why don't you bring him over for dinner so I can see who he is?" No problem!

In the beginning there was a wonderful small group of nearly twelve of us who came to practice with Suzuki-roshi. After *zazen* we would have breakfast together on a table in Mrs. Suzuki's kitchen. Of course, we were trying to be good Zen students, and when I recall those days, it really makes me laugh. The way we acted, we were more like old people. I was twenty-five and some others may have been thirty or forty years old, but we had the idea that to be good Zen students, we had to walk very slowly and be very quiet and always be very well behaved. But that was only my idea. I had such a great misunderstanding of what Zen was that I turned myself into a kind of senior citizen.

Quite a few times Mrs. Suzuki would come into the kitchen with her hair in disarray because she had just awakened, and since this was her kitchen, she would come in to brush her teeth. We were a little bit shocked to see Mrs. Suzuki appear like this just as we were about to have our *oryoki* meal (though we didn't yet have *oryoki* bowls). So she would begin brushing her teeth, and we would pretend that she wasn't there. And then her brushing would become louder and louder, and we were still pretending not to notice, and then she would start gargling! Loud and clear!

There were many of these surprises in the early days, and this is part of the spirit and joy of Zen. Once on April Fools' Day I was the only person who came for morning *zazen*. Suzuki-roshi used to look out the window to see if anyone was coming, and sometimes he would even phone people: "Are you coming?" On this day Mrs. Suzuki met me at the door and said, "Suzuki-roshi just died." I was so shocked and saddened that all I could say was a very sad "Oh!" Then she said, "April Fools'! American custom!" So you can see we had very good training.

There are many stories like these, but what I want you to know is that although what you read in books is some kind of food for thought or imagination, actually Dharma comes from a very deep place of human suffering. If human suffering weren't as bad as it is, there'd be no need for Dharma. I don't mean to make it sound pessimistic or negative, but because there's great suffering, there's also great freedom and great compassion and wisdom. This is what I like about Dharma. From this great suffering comes the beautiful lotus that thrives only from the mud.

That's our practice whether we like it or not; and that also includes whether or not we like the forms of practice. Sometimes I hear people say, "Oh, the form is too difficult." But the forms are essential to help us round the sharp edges we cannot see. When we practice in a group, there are many things that we don't see in ourselves, but others can see them. *Sangha* practice is very beneficial in this way because we help to polish each other. People are usually very self-centered, I'm afraid, and we need some rules and forms in order to smooth these sharp edges within us. As we rub against each other, it's similar to the way a pearl becomes beautifully bright. The more the rubbing . . . it's the brilliance of becoming! This is one definition of *sangha*.

When Mrs. Suzuki visited recently, she told us that her school's lineage comes directly from the great Japanese tea master Rikyu Zenki. Her school is called the Omote school and is closely connected to Zen practice. It seems that many famous people in Japan were attracted to other tea schools, but the Omote school is very simple and down to earth. During one of the last tea ceremonies Mrs. Suzuki offered before returning to Japan, I saw a wild iris opening in the alcove, or *tokonoma,* while she was practicing tea. The *tokonoma* expresses serenity in a very simple way; subtly illuminated, it often has a scroll of some beautiful calligraphy and an elegant flower arrangement. Tea *as it is* affects everything, even the wild iris in its vase. This fact is ordinary Dharma, although if you try to do it, you will find it impossible.

When she was watching and teaching her students, Suzuki-sama would say, "Tom-san, tea has entered your heart." Or, "Bill-san, tea has left your heart." This was our practice. It's hard for us to see ourselves or what we are doing, but the teacher and other people can see us quite easily because they're not blinded by our own view. Our eye cannot see itself.

Even if it cannot see itself, it's okay. Our practice will help it to see, and when it does, universal mind or original mind will reveal itself. This black Zen master's stick that Otogawa-roshi gave me is called *nyo-i,* meaning "everything is okay" or "just like this." This is a very beautiful Zen term. In English "just like this" may be kind of puzzling, but in the context of the Buddhadharma, it is one of the most refined expressions of life: seeing the world as it is, without projection, blame, or judgment. The more I've held this stick and used it, the more I've come to be aware that the wood itself does not *become* polished. It's *already* polished. We have definite ideas about how we'd like things to be; for instance, it's nice to have some wood so you can polish it and make it appear darker, more shiny, or more aged. But actually, your wood is already originally and completely polished *as it is*. It's just for us to see this and to know this; seeing through our own two eyes with the vastness of universal mind, within which all the expansiveness and lightness and joy are rooted. That's Buddha and ancestors' stuff! And that's what our practice of returning to our original quiet and calm is rooted in, so that we can see clearly within ourselves just as we are.

22

DOING FOR THE THING ITSELF

We should work like the rain. The rain just falls. It doesn't ask, Am I making a nice sound down below? Or, Will the plants be glad to see me? Will they be grateful? The rain just falls, one raindrop after another. Millions and billions of raindrops, only falling. This is the open secret of Zen.

THERE ARE MANY translations of the *Sandokai*, the poem we chant every day during our service, written by our great Chinese ancestor Sekito Kisen. It was written more than a thousand years ago, during a time when the two major Zen or Chan schools, known as the Northern and Southern schools, were involved in a great dispute. Each school insisted that it held the true Dharma, and Sekito Kisen observed that both sides were fighting so hard that they were forgetting the Way. It was in response to this circumstance that he wrote the poem.

For many years we've used a translation of the *Sandokai* entitled *The Identity of Relative and Absolute,* but lately I've been calling it *The Intimacy of Relative and Absolute.* Dogen once wrote that enlightenment is just intimacy with all things. Isn't that wonderful? Intimacy with all things. We should understand this phrase deeply because it doesn't just mean that we get close to things or that we like things very much. It's more profound than that. Intimacy is identity, and identity is intimacy. Intimacy carries the same meaning as the words Suzuki-roshi used when describing *shikan taza*: through and through. This is how he encouraged us to sit, to practice, to live, and to die. And this is the meaning of the intimacy, or identity, of relative and absolute. The intimacy of our Big Mind.

In our translation the last two lines of the *Sandokai* are "I respectfully say to those who wish to be enlightened [who wish to be free from yourself], do not waste your time by night or day." The essence expressed by these lines covers everything. It points to a quality of being that comes from our original mind, which is behind the very lives we live. This quality of being is the same as the intimacy I just mentioned. If we don't have this quality, or if we lose it, that will be very regrettable because this is where the juice or the joy of life comes from. One of the reasons Zen has lasted for so many centuries is that it helps us to rediscover, to cultivate, and to retain this quality of being that has been ours from the beginning and that is always available to us whether we are working, sitting *zazen,* or engaged in the many activities of our everyday lives.

Suzuki-roshi translates the final line of the *Sandokai* as "Do not vainly pass through sunshine and shadows." This translation came from his very refined training and poetic mind, but they are not just words, and his direct and powerful presence often demonstrated what they really mean. He would tell us, "Don't goof off!" That's the same as not vainly passing through sunshine and shadows. "Don't goof off!" Sometimes when he said this, it was kind of frightening. He would say it in an almost godlike voice, sometimes with a very stern face and sometimes with a gentle smile. But in either case the profound meaning underlying the words expressed by Sekito Kisen came through.

Roshi had great insight into our dualistic minds, and he would tell us something like this: "Every week I hear people saying how hard they work, how many hours they spend at their job, and how tired they are. Life has become busier and busier. People wake up early, get ready for work, then drive the long commute and put in a nine-, ten-, or even twelve-hour day. After work they get back into traffic, and by the time they're home and need to cook dinner, they're completely exhausted. And then, for some, it's family time! 'I'm always working!' they say. But I don't believe it. I know they are working hard, trying hard at everything they do, this is a given, but even though you work very hard, sometimes you are still passing your valuable time without doing anything. I'm sorry to say it, but it's true."

You are spending your time, but you are not being *spent* by your time in the way Sekito, my great-great-uncle, meant, and there is a big difference. For many people there is no difference between spending time and wasting time. But another way of saying wasting time is killing time, which really means killing yourself, your original mind.

In Zen *this* being, our very own being, *is* time. Time and being are identical, exactly the same. Dogen even wrote that time is *uji*, "time-being." When we say we are spending time, really we are talking about this quality of being and the place within us, the source, from which it is expressed. This is what you should look at when you consider how you are spending your time, because you are also spending this being. The quality of being is being spent.

In Zen or just in life, which means in whatever we do, we are just like a matchstick. First we have to strike the match to ignite it. Then we have to light something with the fire and throw the match away. Strike and ignite it, light something, throw it away. This is an analogy for our whole practice.

One day Ummon, another great southern Chinese Zen ancestor who lived near the temple of the Sixth Ancestor, addressed the *sangha*. "I don't ask you about yesterday," he said. "Nor do I ask you about the day after. Can you say something?" This was Ummon's style of teaching. Everybody in the assembly became silent, and of course their minds began working overtime, which is exactly the wrong direction to follow. To relieve everybody, Ummon said, "Every day is a good day." This koan is more than one thousand years old. How do you understand it? When Suzuki-roshi discussed it, he told us that it doesn't mean that if you had a hard day you should pretend everything was great and not complain. It's fine to complain if you had some difficulty and want to tell your friend that the day was really hard. Maybe you were weighed down with work or the boss was in a bad mood or you forgot to do something. There's nothing wrong with saying, "It was pretty rough today, but it's okay. I can make it." Of course, saying, "It was a hard day and I'm blaming you," is something quite different. But even complaining about the heat or the cold is fine. It's only natural that we do it. "Every day is a good day" points us in a different direction. It means don't waste your time. And not wasting time means knowing how you use your time and how time uses you. By remembering or being aware of this, you will thoroughly rediscover the quality of being that's within yourself.

We need to look with careful attention to see how we are spending our time. For example, more and more I hear people say how busy they are. Even when they're not at work, it's busy, busy, busy. But if you ask them if they are spending their time in vain, they will say, "No. I'm busy all the time!" which reveals that they are, because if you are actually spending your time, and being spent by time, you don't need to say anything. You have nothing to prove or justify; you "just work." The emphasis on the "I" in "I'm busy" is extra. Even if you think to yourself, "I'm working very hard. I'm working for Zen. I'm working for ecology. I'm working to save all sentient beings," it is extra. *Only work.* That's all.

Most people get caught when they think they know what they are actually doing, what the purpose is, or the goal. If you think you really know these things, you may still be doing things in vain, because for most people the purpose is still dualistic. It's based on your evaluation of what's good and what's bad, what's effective or cost efficient or useful or useless, big or small. We get fooled by all these labels, all these names, and it brings a self-consciousness to our activity. Part of the reason we do this is that we want to be good. We want to be real good people. But you already are good, you practice so you can see the basic goodness that you already have. You don't need anyone to tell you that you are a good person, or a good father, mother, sister, or brother. Suzuki-roshi told us, "If you do things because you should do them, then this is real practice." When you hear this, you may say, "That's it? Do things because you should do them and this is real practice?" But whatever you think, it is so.

Our usual way is to bring all of our dualistic thinking, all of our concern with purpose and success, into our activity. But this way only separates us from what we are doing and causes us many problems. We should work like the rain. The rain just falls. It doesn't ask, Am I making a nice sound down below? Or, Will the plants be glad to see me? Will they be grateful? The rain just falls, one raindrop after another. Millions and billions of raindrops, only falling. This is the open secret of Zen. When we sit, we only sit.

When we cook, we only cook. Otherwise we are doing our work and spending our time in vain. Whether you are a Buddhist or not, it doesn't matter. Whether you are in front of a computer, or digging a ditch, or painting with a brush, it doesn't matter. In every area and activity of human life, we can follow the example of the rain. When you do engage your life in this way, when you bring some confidence to it from the foundation you discover in sitting, this is intimacy, this is "quality of being." It is a deep expression of your original nature, and there is no self-consciousness between you and your activity, no second-guessing, no doubt.

Hui Neng, the Sixth Ancestor, said that when you are strong, you turn the Dharma wheel. Being strong means doing things because you should do them, as Suzuki-roshi said, or doing for the thing itself. Then you are free from dualistic considerations. When you do things not because of Buddha, or because of yourself, or because of truth, or even for all sentient beings, but for the things themselves, then that is the true way. It is how we step out of a polarized life, out of the sequence of cause and effect. Of course, you need some strong foundation to help you to stand up, but you already have it, and whether you feel good or bad, when there are things that you should do, you will just do them.

In the *Sandokai* it says, "Each thing has its own virtue." When you just do what you should do, you not only discover *their* virtue, but you discover that their virtue is your virtue, too. Then you encounter the great intimacy where, no matter what you are doing, you are always meeting yourself—your original self-nature. When you understand this kind of feeling of doing for the thing itself, beyond any concept of like and dislike, good or bad, beyond any conditions, you will have returned on your original way, going home.

There are three hundred koans translated by Dogen, and in

the Ninety-first Case a monk asks Sekito Kisen, "What is the meaning of the Buddhadharma?" If you like, you can understand this as "What is the meaning of truth?" Sekito replied, "No gain, no knowing." This is really the key. With no gaining and no knowing, you are just sitting when you sit, only working when you work. This is doing for the thing itself. Nothing else. Then whatever activity you engage in, and wherever you are, you have the same conditions and opportunity to encounter this unconditional experience. No matter what age you are, or what sex you are, or how long you've been practicing, no gaining and no knowing is the key for you to experience the same universal thing. Thinking of the goal won't get you there; you have to lose your self within the activity. You are the activity, and the activity itself has no beginning and no end. When you rake the ground, the ground rakes you. The ground tells you where to rake. The ground tells you how to rake. You become the activity, and the activity becomes you. This is just sitting. This is studying the Dharma for the sake of the Dharma. This is true intimacy. Any thought of gain is extra.

Later in the Case the monk asks Sekito Kisen to say a little bit more, and he responds, "The vast sky is not hindered by the floating white clouds." The vast sky means your essence of mind, the immensity of your sitting practice. The immensity of sitting itself. People often say that sitting is pretty calm and quiet. But those are just the characteristics pointing at sitting. What you experience when you and your sitting become one is the immensity of sitting itself, which is the immensity of the universe. Your own immensity. This is what you experience, and this is what's been handed down nearly twenty-six hundred years. We lose ourselves within the activity. Difficult or not, it's true. Realized or not, believe it or not, it's still true.

When I wrote "Breath Sweeps Mind" in the *enso*, I was expressing the prelude to this intimacy, this immensity that is always with you. With the strong foundation of everyday *zazen* practice, Breath Sweeps Mind releases you and relieves you of your narrow idea of yourself. It makes it possible for you to let go of your idea of what you are doing or why you are doing, whether you are in the *zendo* or in your everyday life. It allows the rain to fall. When you practice Breath Sweeps Mind, you just let go. Even if you let go a little bit, it's okay. This is the utmost kindness we can give to others, which includes ourselves. It is one thing we can definitely give to the whole wide world.

23

SONOMAMA

When you give yourself to practice through and through,
which means through and beyond feelings and thoughts,
little by little you begin to allow something great to
surface, something without beginning or end. That's as it is!

THERE IS SOME HISTORY to the word *sonomama* that I'd like to share with you. During the early 1980s I was corresponding with an American monk who was studying with a Zen master off the coast of the Yellow Sea, near Eihei-ji. In one of his letters he mentioned the word *sonomama* because it was similar to the name of our temple and also because it means "as it is." (The characters for this word and our temple here on Sonoma Mountain are as follows: *so*—"ancestors"; *no*—"capable"; *ma*—"grind and polish"; and then we add *san*—"mountain." These characters are very common and capture the same feeling as our Asian temples.) When I read part of his letter, it unknowingly planted a seed in my mind that was to grow in the coming seasons.

Sometime later I was given a large Japanese high-fashion book with the title *Sonomama*. The meaning of the title given in the book was: "Just like it is; Don't move; As you are; Just like that"; and "Originally so!" Pretty amazing, isn't it? The book was essentially a black-and-white photo essay of just plain simple everyday folks, not models at all, standing within their natural environs while dressed in high-fashion clothing designed by people like Ralph Lauren, Christian Dior, and Paco. There were fishermen standing on the docks, two farm women standing arm in arm in the finely trimmed tea fields, a tattooed truck driver in his proudly overdecorated semi, a full high-fashion suit and derby accompanied by the smiling face of a fifty-year-old man standing on sand dunes. Not one of these people was affected by the clothing they wore. They remained through and through, *as it is*. Their original self did not leave them for one instant. The sad thing, though, is that they do not *recognize* their true nature.

In the Zen world the word *nyo* means "as it is" as well as "just like this." And interestingly enough, the stick that Zen masters often hold, which some people in the West refer to as the "roshi's stick," is called *nyo-i*. One time when the late Kobun Chino Otogawa-roshi was asked, "What is it?" after a very long pause he replied, "It keeps my hand from shaking." There are many authentic ways to express *nyo*. Another time when Otogawa-roshi was asked what the stick symbolized, he simply said, "Everything is okay." That's a very skillful response because if you say anything too philosophical or lofty, people might begin to think about it too much and become confused. So he simply said, "Everything is okay." That expression goes very deep. When people hear it, it makes them feel they can relax because no matter what the conditions may be, there is no difficulty. Isn't this what it's all about?

In essence, both *nyo* and *nyo-i* mean "just like this" or "as it is," so really they are the same. The best way to explain or demonstrate *nyo-i* would be for me to strike my stick on the floor: *Bam!* That's *nyo-i*. Maybe later on, after I did that, we might have some discussion about what we think the meaning is, but as soon as I strike my stick on the floor, you got it, whether you knew it or not. That's *nyo-i* and that's *as it is*. No separation. In your eyes and ears, in your body, in your mind, there is only *nyo-i*.

The ideogram for *i*, which helps to make up the characters for *nyo-i*, includes the word *heart/mind* on the bottom and means "will, intention, or inclination." So we have *as it is* or *just like this* supported by *intention* or *will*. It's also interesting that another word for *okesa*, or Buddha's robe, is *nyo*. This can be found in the word *nyoho-e* where *ho* means "Dharma" and *e* is "robe" or "material." So there we have it again: *as it is*—Buddha's teaching—robe, patch by patch the absolute and relative sewn together. *Nyo-ho-e*. Perhaps, even after this brief description, you can see that when they are naturally received, the precepts and all the teachings in the Buddhadharma eventually lead us to recognize *as it is*.

When Suzuki-roshi gave a talk, he would transmit the most intimate thing to us in a very ordinary way, because this quest of ours is very natural and not difficult, just like the river longing to return to the ocean. It was not just information that was being transmitted, and at the time there wasn't anything like Dharma successors or a great structure in place, but there was a real heart structure. It was through this heart structure that the transmission was made, and it's important to understand that at the root of this heart structure was *nyo*.

In one of his talks, where he was speaking about the sewing of Buddha's robe, he used the words *through and through*, which is another way of expressing *nyo*. In that section he beautifully explained one of the underlying meanings of *through and through*:

> When we say "Buddha's robe," it is just a robe, just a piece of material. When this material is just this material, it is not any particular material. It is part of the universe, not this material.

Because you say this is for a table or a stool, it becomes special. But if this is just this material, then it could be mine, it could be for the Buddha, it could be for you. This is exactly the same practice as your zazen. When you just become you, then that is how that practice or your practice includes everything. When we let or allow this material just to be this material, without say-ing "mine" or "yours," then this material could be for everyone. And it is something more than material to cover a stool.

The material is just the material *through and through,* and therefore it includes everything. Suzuki-roshi always liked to say that we should know everything, including our lives, *through and through.* He was very fond of that expression. And that's the Bodhisattva vow. When we live by it, with a commitment to liv-ing life *as it is,* or *through and through,* we are actually making the vow to include all parts of life, and all parts of our lives, *as it is.* Joy, happiness, loneliness, aggression, sorrow. Life! So when you feel lonely, I'm happy that you feel lonely. And when you feel sad, I'm joyful that you feel sad, because just to know that you are alive and can feel means that "everything is okay." Maybe it sounds a little crazy to say so, but it's wonderful. Then whatever you fear is not so great, the pain is not so great, these are just the conditions of our life, and our practice works to undermine the grip of these conditions. Actually, when you give yourself to practice *through and through,* which means through and beyond feelings and thoughts, little by little you begin to allow some-thing great to surface, something without beginning or end. That's *as it is!* And if you stick to your vow and stay with it, to your surprise something in you will naturally open.

There was a young student from Iceland who came to sit with us for his first *sesshin.* After a few days of keeping the schedule, sitting nine or ten times a day, participating in work practice, eating meals in the *oryoki* ritual form, he realized that the discomfort and pain he was experiencing during the *sesshin* was just pain. Nothing more. (Of course, I don't mean the pain that tells you that you are going to injure yourself.) He was actually very happy and said that he felt he would be able to apply this understanding to his daily life. After the *sesshin* was over, he told us, "Now, because I've experienced so much physical pain, I think I can keep from going back to drugs." Isn't it wonderful? He stayed with it, *through and through,* and found the way to freedom right in the midst of the pain *as it is.*

Each Zen practitioner is an example of this. Before we came to Zen practice, our hand was clenched in a sort of fist, and maybe just our little finger bent open. It was just the little finger, but even that can affect the entire world. You can see this for yourself if you clench your hand and then begin to open your little finger and notice what this does to the other four fingers. Something happens. And in the same way something wonderful comes out of the discipline of sitting. Sometimes you will hate sitting, sometimes you will love sitting, and over time you will have many different relationships to sitting. You will have painful sitting where one year your back aches more and more, and then when that seems to subside, the next year it's your legs, and after you think you are over that, it's your elbow! It's kind of amusing, actually. But if you stay with it, you notice that these things just move through you. Thoughts, feelings, body aches, they're the same. One thing important for us to remember: Everything changes.

When you stay with the practice, however, even though it can be intense, you find that it begins to round off these sharp edges. Once you notice this, you may even ask for more. Give me more! More practice! Load it on! It's really true, because through your experience you begin to develop some very deep kind of faith. You must cultivate a deep kind of faith in the method, in the Dharma, that the Dharma will not fail you. So you cannot rely on anything but this Self. Big Self is the Dharma. There's an old saying that the mind of sentient beings is Dharma. And through your experience in sitting you will find, as I've said, that the Dharma is good in the beginning, good in the middle, and good in the end. Even when it fails you, it does not fail you, because this is only your thought. But for this to be the case takes a kind of courage, the courage to make a leap. Just as a flea makes a leap. A big leap! And it's only a flea!

It all involves relationship. The little flea is so small, but look how far it leaps. We must be prepared to take some risk, to always continue to make these leaps, as great as the leap of a flea. We must have courage enough to do that, even if we don't know where the leap will take us or if it will end. Suzuki-roshi once said:

> There is no end—there is no end in our practice. Because there is no end in our practice, our practice is good. Don't you think so? But usually, you expect our practice could be effective enough to put an end [to] your hard practice. If I say practice hard just two years, then you will be interested in our practice. If I say, you have to practice [your] whole life, then you will be disappointed. "Oh, Zen is not good. Zen is not for me." But if you understand what practice is, and if you are interested in practice, the reason you are interested in practice is the practice is endless. That is why I am interested in Buddhism. There's no end. If there is some end, I don't think Buddhism is so good. There is no end. Even if human beings vanished from this earth,

Buddhism exists. That is why I am interested in Buddhism. Buddhism is not always perfect. It is not perfect at all. Because it is not perfect, I like it. If it is perfect, someone will be—many people will be interested in it, so there is no need for me to work on it. Because people are very much discouraged with Buddhism, I feel someone must practice Buddhism.

That's Suzuki-roshi's mind. Isn't it wonderful? It's the same mind that would buy the old vegetables when he went to the market because otherwise those vegetables would be thrown away and no one would eat them. That was his way. Toward the latter part of Suzuki-roshi's life he realized that he didn't have much time, and when he gave talks, he would strike his stick on the lectern quite often. Sometimes people would ask him a question, and he would say, "This is the answer," and then he'd strike his stick down sharply. *Nyo!* You got it! But I didn't necessarily understand what he meant every time he did it. I thought, "Maybe Roshi has gone mad or something," because what happens is much more subtle than we can think. *Through and through. As it is.* Live. Die. Buy old vegetables. *Nyo!* Unseen and *before* we can think. Please enjoy your only life!

24

A LOTUS IN
YOUR GARDEN

We cannot separate suffering from enlightenment. Don't forget, we are enlightened from our delusions. So, too, it takes mud for the lotus to become itself, and the greater the mud in your life, the greater the lotus blossom.

WHEN WE PRACTICE TOGETHER by laying aside our dualistic thinking, which usually demands all of our attention, we allow the depth of our existence to begin to surface. Before this summer's practice period began, I had a secret wish that the lotuses we had planted in the pond would bloom. And sure enough, just as the corn in the garden is growing every day, the lotuses in the pond are beginning to bloom right along with our own unknowing blossoming. At an earlier time my secret wish was just to be able to see the lotus. I longed to see and experience it because, as you know, in Dharma it is a special kind of mystical flower—the very prize! When I was in China, just before the tragedy of Tiananmen Square, I saw the leaves of the lotus, but I didn't see the flower. And when we went to Japan, I saw some beautiful flowers in a garden pond and said, with a lot of excitement, "Those look like lotus!" But my hosts told me, "No, they look like lotus, but they aren't lotus." And to tell the truth, that was good to find out because this is part of knowing lotus.

Some plants resemble the lotus, for instance the water lily. But lotuses are not water lilies, and we are not water lilies. We are *lotus,* pure one hundred percent lotus. Water lilies are a beautiful flower, but their leaf shape is different from that of lotus leaves, which are very large and almost perfectly round, so large and round that when Hoitsu Suzuki-roshi was here one time, he kiddingly took the dried lotus leaf off the wall of the *dokusan* room and put it on his head. It was large enough to be a rain hat! Water lilies have indentations on their leaves, and the flower is small and quite beautiful, too. The lily flower rests on the surface of the water, whereas the lotus grows out of the mud and stands above the water. Traditionally, the lotus is a Mahayana symbol of wisdom and compassion because it needs the mud in order to grow into a beautiful and mysterious flower. And so do we.

We cannot separate suffering from enlightenment. Don't forget, we are enlightened from our delusions. So, too, it takes mud for the lotus to become itself, and the greater the mud in your life, the greater the lotus blossom. The lotus can reach the surface of the water eight or ten feet above the pond's floor. As it sends out stems, the large leaf appears vertically above the surface and begins to unfold its round self. At some point the lotus flower itself begins blooming from within the leaf area, and it stands with a quiet dignity three feet high above the water. I've even seen lotuses here standing four to five feet, maybe higher. The blossoms here are about as large as your head. Their white and pinkish life span is four to five days, and each evening they close their petals and go to sleep. At some point all the petals drop off into the pond as the roundish pod continues to grow in size. In time it becomes so large and heavy with its own weight that the tall stem bends and returns the seeds to the pond's rich and muddy field.

Life is really so wonderful. Of all the places I read about the lotus, the lotus we were to receive here at Sonoma Mountain was in the Valley of the Moon, just down the road where the mountain meets the valley. A Chinese doctor had grown lotuses in a pond across the Valley of the Moon for a restaurant. After reading about it in the newspaper, I became very excited and phoned him immediately. "You've got to help us!" I said. "We are a Buddhist temple!" And he spontaneously said, "Yes." I also asked, "Do you think the lotus will grow here?" And he said, "Only the Buddha knows!" When I heard this, I recalled asking Mahaghosananda, "How do you grow lotus?" He said, "Just wrap the seed in the mud and throw them into the pond."

Dr. Wu kindly cut a few tubers for us and we planted them all in the pond. We did it just last year, which was a difficult drought year that caused the pond's water to recede. I was worried, but it is said that as long as the roots are wrapped in mud, the lotus lives. And this year, because of the rains, we have water, and the lotuses have begun to bloom.

I was laughing at myself: "You looked all over for lotuses, but where they are found is in your own backyard." This is very important. The Dharma usually points out that it's always near at hand, or as Suzuki-roshi said, "It's always with you, whether you realize it or not—Buddha Nature is always with you." My deepest wish, and the great gift for all of you, is that you become aware of your own lotus. Then, as you cultivate the seasons of your awareness, your lotus will surely bloom. Please come to Sonoma Mountain to enjoy the lotuses and to hear the wondrous sound of lotus leaves flapping in the wind!

25

THINGS AS IT IS

*We practice this by simply investigating what is behind
everything: the thoughts of the thinker (where do they
actually come from?), the sound you just heard, the cup
you just saw. This investigation may be made using all six
senses. As you continue this investigation, you will find
that there is nothing behind "behind." There is nothing to
see, and yet something has been seen, otherwise it couldn't
be recognized.*

ONE TIME AT TASSAJARA we were visited by a Zen
master named Tatsugami. He was the *ino* at Eihei-ji,
which means he was the head of the *zendo* responsible
for the spirit, training, and discipline of Zen practice there. He
was also a very tough guy. Physically he was very, very strong,
and we were told that because he was so strong, sometimes people would challenge him to a fight. And the thing is, if they
wanted to fight him, he would say okay and fight them. It makes
me laugh, because here's a monk who fought sumo wrestlers and
other people who wanted to prove themselves against him. Not
exactly your image of a Zen teacher, is it? But he met what presented itself right there in front of him, so maybe there's something to it.

While he was at Tassajara, Tatsugami introduced the expression *menmitsu no kafu,* which I've mentioned before. This term is very important for those of us who practice the Soto way. Suzuki-roshi said that *menmitsu nokafu* means "being very careful in doing things" and "being very considerate." It also may imply embodying your teacher's character, expression, and depth. During Tatsugami's time as visiting teacher at Tassajara, he made this phrase come alive.

The reason we practice *menmitsu no kafu* is not so that we can be known as nice or good people. Even if someone challenges us to a fight, we still can practice it. So we have to look a bit deeper to discover what it's all about. In Zen we say that you may find everything within your own mind. You don't have to look in the dictionary or on the bookshelf. You don't have to look outside yourself. Nothing is missing right here within you, but you don't know it, so you are constantly looking outside, far and near, left, right, and behind. But right here, where you are and as you are, you can find everything within. This is an understanding essential to Zen, and it is also at the very root of *menmitsu no kafu* and all the ways in which we express it, including placing your shoes together outside the *zendo,* folding your clothes in your room, working with utensils in the kitchen or tools in the garden, practicing *zazen,* and living your daily life with people in the world. These are some of the various ways of practicing *zazen.* They are an expression of your Big Self, your Big Mind, which includes everything; *menmitsu no kafu* is not just a matter of being careful and polite. Once you realize this, you will see how *menmitsu no kafu* is a natural expression of recognition and gratitude rooted in this spacious and wondrous Big Mind.

There's another Zen phrase I've mentioned that Suzuki-roshi used and that is very much a part of what I've been discussing:

things as it is. He would tell us that part of our practice was to "observe *things as it is.*" It's difficult to explain precisely what *things as it is* means, but it includes seeing things without imposing any judgments or projections or placing any particular screen in front of yourself. For example, for almost thirty years at our temple we have practiced an all-night sitting during *Rohatsu,* which commemorates the Buddha's enlightenment. The very first night I decided we would all sit from twelve to four o'clock in the morning out of respect for Shakyamuni Buddha's enlightenment on December 8 and Suzuki-roshi's memorial December 4. The *doan* rang the bell three times to begin the long-night sitting, and I got into full lotus posture. Then five minutes later *ding!* the bell rang to end the sitting. I had sat four hours and didn't even know it. It seemed like no more than five minutes had passed. So every year after that I tried to do the same thing, and I was completely defeated. As you can imagine, these long sittings varied from my feeling disturbed, anxious, restless, and angry, with all kinds and senses of "loss" accompanied by the usual fatigue and sleepiness. But this is what the training should do to you—defeat you, defeat your thoughts, defeat your idea for the preservation of yourself. And yet despite this we continue to sit.

From this experience we can see that one of the meanings of *things as it is* is that you have to give up and surrender to the moment. I wanted my sitting during *Rohatsu* to be a certain way, but it never was. Doesn't that happen sometimes in your own life? We want things to go a certain way, we want our lives to be a certain way, but it's not what's appearing. I'm sorry to have to say this, but I'm afraid it's really so. What appears is just what comes right there in front of you, and that's your life *as it is.* If you don't accept it, you will end up fighting your own life, which causes a great deal of suffering. But when you begin to actively accept it, something changes. The whole struggle is when we refuse to accept what's right there, when we refuse to surrender.

The best way to explain *things as it is* is for me to strike my stick on the floor: *Bam!* That's *things as it is.* That demonstrates it; Zen is demonstration and direct experience. But still there is some need for explanation. In one of his talks on this subject Suzuki-roshi says, "We are not necessarily observing everything as-it-is. We say, 'Here is my friend, there's the mountain, or there's the moon.' But as soon as we say that, the mountain is no longer a mountain. It's that mountain over there, and the moon is that moon over there. You think your friend is your friend. The moon, you think, is the moon, but it is not actually the moon itself, or your friend himself, or the mountain itself. You think, 'Here I am and there is the mountain.' In this case, when you observe things in that way, it is a dualistic way of observing: 'Here am I. There is the mountain.' This is our usual understanding of life."

But it is not the Buddhist understanding of life. In our way of observing things *menmitsu no kafu* is the natural expression that results from seeing our original heart/mind. When we are very careful and considerate as we observe *things as it is,* we find the mountain or the moon or our friend right here within ourselves because we ourselves are the Big Mind within which everything exists.

When the late Katagiri-roshi's mother died, he was only fourteen years old. He cried and cried because he wanted her to come back, but no matter how much he cried, he couldn't make her come back. Finally, he understood this truth, and then he cried even more until he realized that his mother was right there in his heart. She was still right there. So she left, and at the same time she didn't leave. Nothing leaves. Our idea is that the moon is over there and I'm over here. But the Buddha's way is that the moon is here; mother is here; father is here; everybody's here. This is what is meant by "the Big Mind includes everything."

There's a student in Poland who stole some bread when she was a little girl. She was with a little boy when she did it, and after they stole the bread, they ran away as fast as they could because the Nazis were already chasing them. It's such a sad story because as the soldiers caught up with them, she hid under a train and watched as the soldiers shot the little boy. She witnessed the whole thing, and it remains very deep in her mind. She feels enormous guilt and remorse for what happened. She also feels that if she forgives that episode, then all the people who met similar fates will be forgotten. But it doesn't have to be forgive-and-forget. There's a way you can forgive and remember, because it remains right here in your heart. It's actually pretty difficult to just erase something. But we can work with things because they stay right here. There's a kind of denial that goes along with forgive-and-forget, but forgive-and-remember has an honor and dignity within it. And the Big Mind or Big Self that includes everything makes it possible for us to see *things as it is* and work with them because, in actuality, we find them right here within ourselves.

When we say "right here," we should be clear that it's Big Self we are talking about, Big Mind, not the small mind that believes that you are here and the mountain is far away in the distance or the moon is floating in the sky. Suzuki-roshi made a clear distinction between seeing things with Big Mind and finding things out with our small mind. In general, small mind refers to the mind that is under limitation—for instance, under the influence of our self-centered thoughts. It is often based on some particular emotional understanding we may have or some discriminating thought that separates the Oneness of life and says instead, "Here I am, and there is the mountain. This is good, and that is bad. This is too long, and that is too short." In this case, even though you think you are observing *things as it is,* actually you are not. Why? Because your discriminating thoughts, impulses, and desires obstruct the way. Our practice is very much about letting go of this kind of emotional or intellectual discrimination or prejudice, which separates things according to the needs and habits of small mind.

We practice this by simply investigating what is behind everything: the thoughts of the thinker (where do they *actually* come from?), the sound you just heard, the cup you just saw. This investigation may be made using all six senses. As you continue this investigation, you will find that there is nothing behind "behind." There is nothing to see, and yet something has been seen, otherwise it couldn't be recognized. This recognition is our pure and natural awareness; it is not mind-made. This is the "nonthing" that can recognize *things as it is.*

When our inherent, pure awareness is turned on, without any effort thoughts vanish so that no-thoughts can exist in this spaciousness. Therefore we are free from samsara and karma. We should learn to rest lightly in this pervasive space, focusing neither inwardly nor outwardly. Resting means what it says—with no effort, lightly and loosely in this space that pervades the whole universe. The Zen practice is to repeat this over and over again until you become intimate with it. It is not a difficult thing to do because you are already doing it. It's just that you haven't recognized it. The difference between Buddhas, Bodhisattvas, and human beings is that Buddhas and Bodhisattvas recognize and know the nature of mind.

When Suzuki-roshi was teaching me how to write the character *do,* as in the chant *Sandokai,* he said, "This means 'same.' We're same. *Do!* We're both the same." Even though *that's* Suzuki-roshi and *this* is Bill Kwong, because our essence is originally one, we're the same. That's *do.* After we practiced the character together, it was hard for me to tell which one was Suzuki-roshi's and which was mine.

Do could mean "emptiness" and also "oneness" or "intimacy." And this "intimacy" means one whole body, or Big Mind; your Big Mind. Despite the fact that our thinking mind has separated us from one another—countries, families, people all living as if we were originally separate and apart—Big Mind means that *originally* we are one and that the many different things we encounter are just many expressions of this one, whole big being.

When we live our lives rooted in this understanding, something may be big or it may be small. If it's big, okay, it's big; and if it's small, it's small. There's no need to make comparisons. This is just *things as it is,* and this is life-giving. All of these seemingly separate things exist, and yet everything is within yourself: the trees, the breeze, the sky, the heat, the little boy, the piece of bread. Everything is one. Actually, it's your realization experience. You may be looking out the window, and the glass disappears and the bamboo you were looking at is you. That's the physical sensation you have. We can't even call it experience because experience means subject and object, so it is *before.* And afterward we say, "That was *wonder-full!*" Before thought is *things as it is.* It helps if we continually remind ourselves that *we are originally one.* And that's why we practice, because there is no other way to cultivate this Dharma truth that is beyond thought. Little by little over the many seasons, this cultivation undermines our false ideas until they begin to lose their grip on us. Ultimately, this practice leads to complete liberation.

26

THE DEAD FAWN

It may be that our idea that no self is beyond everything is not enough. It could be that the awareness and compassion of tears is a way of helping people.

ONE OF THE MOST FAMOUS Korean monks, who lived around thirteen hundred years ago during the Silla period, was a man named Won Hyo. When he was a young man, there was a terrible civil war in his country and he saw a great amount of suffering. Many homes were burned, people's lives were destroyed, and many of his own friends were killed. As a result of all he witnessed, Won Hyo made up his mind to become a monk. He shaved his head and went off to the mountains, where he practiced meditation, chanting, reading the sutras, and keeping the precepts. He did this for quite some time, practicing wholeheartedly every day, but despite all of his effort he realized that his deep quest, his life question, was still not answered. Since there was a tradition of a walking spirit in those days, he decided he would set out upon the road and walk to China.

One day as Won Hyo was walking, he noticed that night was nearing, and since he felt very tired, he found a place where he might safely rest and went to sleep. In the middle of the night, however, he woke up and felt a terrible thirst. He knew he had to quench this thirst, but it was pitch black and he didn't know where he was. Of course, there were no flashlights, and he had no matches or anything else to help light his way, so he got on his hands and knees and began to search along the ground for some water. Finally, there in the dark, his hand happened upon a cup, and he felt so happy he thought, "How wonderful! The Buddha has provided me with a cup." But that was not all, because as he picked up the cup, he realized that it held something within it. Immediately he began to drink, and it was so delicious that Won Hyo thought he had never tasted such pure delicious water before. "Gee," he said to himself, "I must be a pretty good practitioner for the Buddha to provide me with such wonderful water exactly when I need it."

In the morning, when Won Hyo awakened, he saw that the cup he had used the night before was really a skull and that inside the skull there were maggots and insects and blood, which was what he had been drinking. Of course, his mind immediately began to race with a million thoughts and feelings until he became so nauseated that he started to vomit. And as soon as he vomited, his mind opened, and he realized that it is dualistic understanding that causes good and bad, life and death; and that when there is no dualistic thinking, there is no Buddha, no Zen, no Dharma. There's nothing, and this nothingness is also emptiness, magnificently quiet and calm, suffused with awareness. Actually, Won Hyo realized that dualistic thinking is people's universal master. I don't mean that clear thinking is, but deluded, conditioned thinking is everyone's universal master. When he realized this, he decided there was no need for him to continue walking to China, and so he turned around and walked back to Korea.

After returning to Korea, Won Hyo became a very famous Pure Land priest, and many people came from across the land to receive his Dharma, which was that all men and women can be reborn in paradise. But one day, despite his realization and his fame, he knew that he still was not quite satisfied, that his life-and-death question had still not been resolved. He had heard that there was a venerable old Zen master living in a cave not very far away, and so he went to visit the master.

As he approached the master's cave, he heard someone crying from inside. He entered the cave and was shocked to find the old Zen master sitting beside a dead fawn, which was clearly the cause of his grief and tears. The reason Won Hyo was shocked was that he thought that if a person was enlightened, they were beyond feeling; they were beyond sadness and even beyond happiness. He asked the Zen master, "Why are you crying? And what has happened to cause this fawn to die?"

The old master told Won Hyo that some hunters had come through the woods and killed the fawn's mother, leaving the fawn alone. He had come upon the fawn sometime later and had brought it into the cave to care for it. But he didn't know how to keep it alive. The fawn was so young it needed milk, but he couldn't just go to the village and tell the people he needed some milk for an animal, so he made up a story that he needed some milk for his baby son. When they heard this, some people gave him milk without the slightest hesitation, but most others thought it was scandalous that a true monk should have a child. And little by little this feeling spread throughout the village until no one in the village would give him milk except one person, who was only able to offer a small amount. The old master was grateful for even this little bit of milk, but by the time he brought the milk back to the cave, it was too late. The fawn had died.

"But," he told Won Hyo, "my mind is the same mind as that of the fawn. I want milk . . . I need milk . . . I want milk."

We should look carefully at this story. It may be that our idea that no self is beyond everything is not enough. It could be that the awareness and compassion of tears is a way of helping people to be reborn in paradise. It's more human than we think. Therefore when everyone is sad, we are sad, and when everyone is happy, we are also happy. This is the Way. The emotions are very clear, and because the emotions are so clear, it's similar to when you go backstage in a theater after a moving performance; you will see that the actors, actresses, and dancers are like the fading leaves in an autumn vineyard; they are spent, used up, but because they are used up, they become very real and soft, very soft and open.

27

SHIKAN TAZA: SITTING QUIETLY AND DOING NOTHING

If we do each thing through and through, as Roshi often said, then all of our activities have the possibility of including everything. You will find the stick in the fan and the fan in the stick. You will find the roshi *in your sitting, and you will find yourself in the* roshi, *or in the mountain, or in the garden. When you are working there, that is garden* shikan taza; *when you are cooking, that is cooking* shikan taza. *And that is just being yourself.*

RAISING THE ZEN STICK, raising a finger, raising a fan is all *shikan taza*. In the Dark Ages of Europe there was a term people used, "participating consciousness." It may not be exactly the same thing, but it's pretty similar to *shikan taza*. This subject is not exclusively Asian. It's universal, and it is within each one of us. We are all inherently endowed with this greatest treasure, but it does not mean anything if it is not recognized.

Suzuki-roshi gave a talk in 1968 at Tassajara about *shikan taza*.

I'll include parts of that talk here and make some comments. At the beginning of the talk Suzuki-roshi says, "I want to explain *shikan taza.*" It is unusual for a Zen master to explain something, because Zen depends much upon demonstration and example, but as I quote from his talk, you'll see how a Zen master explains, because we can neither talk about reality nor explain it.

"I want to explain *shikan taza,* which means just to sit. Some monk said to a Zen master, 'It is very hot. How is it possible to sit somewhere where there is no hot or no cold weather?'" This is just like our lives. How can we avoid difficulty? How can we always have a good day? This koan is more than a thousand years old, and yet it is so relevant and familiar. It is our everyday question: How can we avoid being too hot or too cold?

"The master answered, 'When it is hot you should be hot Buddha. When it is cold you should be cold Buddha.' This is Dogen-zenji's understanding of the story. In the actual story the master said, 'When it is hot you should kill hot. When it is cold you should kill cold.'"

There is another Zen saying about this word *kill:* When a Buddha is walking before you on the path, you should kill the Buddha. Of course, this doesn't mean that you should physically kill someone. It means you should kill the *idea* of Buddha because you are Buddha, too. In this story it is the same with hot and cold. Suzuki-roshi continues to explain:

"When it is hot you should kill hot. When it is cold you should kill cold. But if you say kill, the kill is extra. If you say attain enlightenment, the attain is extra. Dogen was very direct when he said, 'When it is hot you should be hot Buddha. When it is cold you should be cold Buddha.'" This is what *shikan taza* means: to be completely within the presence of yourself no matter what the environment. It takes a lot of training and practice, but the benefits are immeasurable, not only for yourself but in the effect it has upon many other people as well.

In *Zen Mind, Beginner's Mind* Suzuki-roshi talks about the stages of practice in the Theravada and Mahayana schools. He says, "The best way is just to do it without having any joy in it, not even spiritual joy." He's talking here about the fourth or highest stage of your sitting practice; there's no joy. That's hard to believe. But when we are sitting, we have to go beyond the source of joy. We can't stop at joy or bliss because this source-less source is where everything comes from and where everything returns. Suzuki-roshi says that at this stage the way is just to do it, forgetting your physical and mental feelings, which basically are your thoughts. You're beyond thought. Forgetting this conditioned you is what "participating consciousness" means—merging with your original mind, which is no other than your inherent pure-bright awareness, or Buddha Nature, which pervades the whole universe.

The next highest stage, the third stage, is just to have physical joy in your practice. When you sit down, you feel a tremendous sense of stability, just like a mountain. It feels like you could sit for a long, long time, so your sitting includes a physical sense of pleasure and joy in its imperturbability. This is a manifestation that your mind and body have merged.

At the second stage, you experience both mental and physical joy. Your sitting is pleasurable, a good feeling pervades you, and it is accompanied by a sense of calm. The result is that you want to sit again and again because you want to create this sense of calm that you had never experienced before, but be aware, you need to remind yourself not to get stuck here.

The first stage is when to a certain extent you have no thinking, and you experience an "undistracted feeling" for things.

There seems to be no curiosity outside of your sitting practice. Your body and mind feel whole and integrated because of the posture, and so there is no need for you to think. By entrusting your existence to your breath and posture, your pulse begins to slow, and your mind waves begin to dissolve. In Theravada practice this is where *sati* may be encountered. The mind is fixed, unwavering, ignited moment to moment in the present. There's no thought or curiosity about anything. There are no obstacles. You are just there on your seat. When you are in this space, anything can ignite your mind: the smell of incense, the rustling sound of a kimono as someone walks behind you in the *zendo,* the stillness of the room. When the mind is ignited again, that's *sati,* which naturally leads one into *samadhi,* whose function is an unwavering focus on your original mind. As you can see, everyone has access to *samadhi* because it is a universal quality of human beings. It does not belong exclusively to some special people or religion.

With *samadhi* your mind enters the highest stage, which is returning the light to its source. Within this empty source is awareness alone. Sometimes it is called the Great Samadhi. In *sati,* which is fixed and calm, the mind merges into the river of *samadhi.* It's a very subtle thing, all part of one rainbow, and can occur only when we go beyond the limitations and conditions of the thought of self and body. When this occurs, wisdom and compassion naturally and simultaneously arise.

There are people who like *sati* and *samadhi.* They like being calm, but they don't like to see people. This is because their *sati* or *samadhi* has not yet reached wisdom and compassion, which is the fourth stage—the emptiness of things. These people like to sit by themselves; they're attached to this pleasurable calmness. This may sound good to some people, but it is not Zen.

It took long years of practice for me to clearly identify all these stages. Calmness is part of the pleasure and joy, but beyond that is a greater calm where you're neither happy nor sad, where you can be free from duality—big/small, hot/cold, dark/light. The Middle Way goes beyond all of these conditions.

The most important thing in these four stages is that they are practiced with no idea of gaining anything. How can you do something with no gaining idea? We are trained to always seek some advantage, so it may seem impossible, but the truth is we do it. For instance, when treading water, the more you try, the quicker you sink. But there's some moment where you forget what you're doing. You stop thinking and just do it. When this occurs, there's a spaciousness, and right there in that spaciousness is forgetting about gain. That's when buoyancy appears, and surprisingly you begin to float.

"When your practice is not good, you are a not-good Buddha. When your practice is good, you are good-Buddha." In other words, you're just who you are. There's really no reason to compare with anyone else, or even with yourself. Such comparisons are based on a gaining idea. But Suzuki-roshi tells us, "Poor and good are Buddhas themselves. Poor is Buddha and good is Buddha and you are Buddha also. Whatever you think or say, every word becomes Buddha. 'I am Buddha.' I is Buddha and am is Buddha and Buddha is Buddha. Buddha. Buddha. Buddha. Buddha. Buddha. Whatever you say. There are no problems."

This is the Zen master's explanation. I hope it puzzles and delights you, too. Somewhere in between our understanding and not understanding is the way. That's what we call faith. Someone once told me Thich Nhat Hanh said that perception is delusion, and that means consciousness is also delusion because the "I" remains unknown. What is this "I"? What is this "I" that does or does not understand? ("Does not understand" is closer because this mind is reaching its limitation.) This is not a new question. It's old, but somehow we avoid it because it is too difficult. And the more it is explained, the further we are from the Dharma.

"There is no need to be bothered with fancy explanations of Buddhism. Everything is Buddha: sitting is Buddha, lying down is Buddha, each word is Buddha. If you say Buddha-BuddhaBuddhaBuddha, that is our way. That is *shikan taza*. When you practice *zazen* with this understanding, that is true *zazen*.

"When you sit you know what Dogen means without thinking or without expecting anything, and when you accept yourself as an awakened person or understand everything as an unfolding of the absolute teaching, the truth, the First Principle, or as part of this Great Being or mystery, when you reach this understanding, whatever you think or see is the actual teaching of Buddha, and whatever you do is the actual practice of Buddha."

This is really so wonderful. It is a kind of sketch of someone who is completely free within the daily activity of their lives. This is *shikan taza* in everyday life, and this is a real Zen person.

According to Suzuki-roshi, there are three ways that problems arise. One is that you *try* to do something. Just as in the example of treading water, you have to try, an effort must be made, but if you try too much, it doesn't work. You have to try and then let go and forget all about the self. Forget all about gain. Then you will discover the buoyancy that was there all the time. If you try to do something, or if you try too hard, you will expect something in return. Acting without any gaining idea is very important because as long as you expect something, you will get discouraged and quit practicing. We should practice with what some people have called "an effortless effort."

The second way problems arise is when you think that nothing will result from your activity. We usually feel unworthy, and do you know, that's ego! It tends to make one become more resigned and passive and is actually the opposite of trying. It can be a very subtle thing to notice about yourself, but it is a common cause of people giving up on their practice.

The third way problems arise is when you feel that you can rely on something. This is really important. We all want some kind of security, whether it is monetary, physical, or spiritual. But you can't even rely on Zen. It is a very good teaching—true, simple, and direct. We want something perfect, something that will always be there for us, but there is no such thing as perfect. The saying "The Dharma is good in the beginning, the Dharma is good in the middle, the Dharma is good in the end" sounds like the Dharma can't fail you, right? Of course, it would be good if we knew what Dharma is, but this saying reminds me of the Buddha's last teaching, last Dharma: You are the light, Dharma is the light; do not rely on any other. I say this because when you do, eventually you will fall down and become very discouraged.

Suzuki-roshi gave a very serious talk during an intensive retreat about how Buddhism is dying in Japan just as Catholicism is dying in the West. It follows a universal cycle of contraction and expansion that applies to all things. At the time Suzuki-roshi wasn't very well, and he shouted, "Death is one of the greatest teachers." He punctuated this with a very strong and clear voice by urging his students: *Don't move!*

This is dying. Something must die—our gaining idea, our idea about relying on something. We should know that there is nothing outside of this Self, which includes the moon, the stars, and the mountains. So the Self we can rely on includes the whole universe; it is not the limited, dualistic or conditioned self.

Maybe sometimes you can't even rely on that, because it may only be an idea and hasn't yet been fully digested. Suzuki-roshi's favorite Zen words were "It's not always so." That means everything is changing and you can't rely on something other than yourself, your real self, or Big Mind, which is before everything.

When you begin to study Zen, you may think you go beyond thoughts and feelings, but the truth is that you become more and more human. It's like with fear and anger: You feel them *through and through,* and because you do feel them in this way, you don't need to dwell on them and aren't caught by them. In this practice you're able to experience the whole spectrum of human emotions by experiencing them, and therefore you can let them go. It's a great misunderstanding to think that feelings are somehow forbidden. We let them come, and we are with them, and also we let them go. Roshi liked to say that the teaching, or the Dharma, is always right here. Even in our feelings, it's always right here.

Suzuki-roshi goes on to talk about how holding any idea of attainment, or making progress in practice, can create some problems. He says, "You may give up if you feel you haven't made any progress after practicing one or two months. But true religion cannot be obtained by seeking for something good."

This is a very true statement because we want to become good. It's one of the things that brings people to practice. But as I've said again and again, we already are good. That's the teaching in the Buddhadharma. It's our wisdom seeking wisdom that brings us and sustains us. As we practice, we rediscover our basic goodness that is always here. There's no other way. This other approach, where we practice with the hope of attaining something, is actually very materialistic, but it is how some people pursue their spiritual practice. "The way to work on spiritual things is quite different," Roshi tells us. "Even to talk about spiritual things is not spiritual but a kind of substitute."

When we rely on anything, when we approach our practice or any part of our lives with this gaining idea or the desire to attain, we are just sowing the seeds of suffering. Anything that appears will disappear. That is Dharma, a universal law. Suzukiroshi says this in a way that may be shocking to some of you: "That you are here means that you will vanish." The fact that we are here means that we will not be here sometime. But we can look at it from a different angle than we usually do. It's not just that we die. Of course, physically we all will die. But while we are alive, our mind can forget the self, which is what I mean when I say that we will not be here. The conditions of greed, anger, and ignorance, and our attachment to them, can die while we are alive. Delusion vanishes from cultivating our awareness. Roshi calls this *seeing through and through*. Isn't it wonderful?

"That you are here means that you will vanish. Things which exist are bound to vanish, and things which you attain cannot be perpetually retained. *Only something which exists before everything else appears exists forever.* [These are my italics.] As long as you seek for something, you will only get the shadow of reality. Only when you do not seek for enlightenment will you find it, and only when you don't strive for something, will you have it. Because you try to attain something, you lose it."

We should realize this very quickly because life is short. How does it work? The more you try to keep something, the more you will suffer because, without fail, it will disappear. For example, everyone wants to be happy, but the more we want to be happy, the more unprepared we are when the inevitable unhappiness arrives. This is because of a big and very common misunderstanding. Sadness and happiness are both part of our lives. It's true for everyone. But they are not opposites. Happy and sad are like the sun and the moon. They share the same sky. So if you are attached to being happy, then you will become very sad. Suzuki-roshi explains:

"Because A tries to be C or D, there are problems. A is just A and A is bound to disappear and that is renunciation." By renunciation Suzuki-roshi means that the self vanishes or disappears into the present moment. "A is just A and when A is just A, [this conditioned self disappears]. To have renunciation is to go beyond the various forms and colors."

In the moment when we go beyond this form, this color, this shape—beyond what we usually think of as ourselves—we don't know who we think we are. We only know afterward. We have this tremendous energy and tears of joy, but while they are occurring, we don't know who we think we are. This is called *only-don't-know* mind. But if someone were near you at this time, they might know or have a sense of who you are. This kind of renunciation, this kind of disappearance, is beyond form and color.

"We have full appreciation of form and color but they are bound to disappear and we should not be attached to that. We do not give them up but accept that they go away; that is renunciation." We're not turning our back to the world, or giving up on the things of the world, but we accept that they do disappear. This is renunciation, but this same world that we live in a long, long time becomes very spacious, juicy, full of life!

"If A always tries to remain A, that is attachment which does not exist in reality." Most people live this way, but that's not reality and that's not renunciation.

"A should just be A and should vanish in the form of C or D. But C or D should not try to be something different from C or D."

In Zen you find something you can't rely on. There are no guarantees, although there is some great being within ourselves that we must try to rediscover so that our life-force is activated. And this is at the core of our practice. At the same time that's not a promise either. In the Genjo Koan it says, in essence, "Some may, some may not." But nevertheless there is something here. We long to be in touch with it and know it's not outside ourselves.

"Only when A is A, only when we satisfy ourselves as A, as I, is there a chance to have renunciation, a chance to vanish or to become one with reality. If A could be something else, then A might be a perpetual being, an eternal being. But no such being exists according to the Dharma.

"Only when A is just A is it possible for A to vanish. Something which exists must vanish. Is there something which does not? If you don't vanish, you are just a ghost." We don't believe in ghosts, but we do not deny the activity of ghosts. The ghosts want to come back. Usually Japanese ghosts have no legs, they can neither stand up nor walk, but they still long to return to experience the life of reality.

So we say "just sit," or "A is A." That's *shikan taza*, just sit. This directly points out liberation from A—when A is just A, or when we just sit, I become free from my idea of myself, free from the *roshi*, completely free of free. This is a great breath of fresh space, to be liberated from yourself.

"You only lose your reality because you try to be something else. Do you understand? I should just try to be A, just myself. Then I have freedom, enlightenment. And I'm not a ghost. I exist here. I may become Buddha himself. This is not some fancy teaching. No teaching could be more direct than just to sit down. You cannot say anything about it, not even yes or no. But this is not something you should believe in because I say so or because Buddha says so. This is the truth which is waiting for you to find it. And it is the only way to attain renunciation without causing any problems for yourself or anyone else. Just to be yourself is no problem whatsoever. This is what is meant by *just to sit*. Zen masters who practice the Rinzai way may give you a koan *mu* instead of telling you *just to sit*. But what is *mu*? *Mu* is *just to sit*. There is no difference and *just to sit* itself will be various kinds of koans for you. There may be thousands of koans for us and *just to sit* includes them all."

This all-inclusiveness, where A is just A, is not limited to sitting, it is the foundation of our practice. It is because of this that I can say that raising the stick, raising the fan, raising a finger is *shikan taza*. We should not be fooled by what appears to be the limits of our activity. If we are thoroughly, intimately present in each thing we do, if we do each thing *through and through,* as Roshi often said, then all of our activities have the possibility of including everything. You will find the stick in the fan and the fan in the stick. You will find the *roshi* in your sitting and you will find yourself in the *roshi,* or in the mountain, or in the garden. When you are working there, that is garden *shikan taza*; when you are cooking, that is cooking *shikan taza*. And that is just being yourself.

Do you understand? Despite the fact that it cannot really be explained, if you understand something that exists before everything appears, your understanding is "sitting quietly and doing nothing." This is the true liberation and renunciation of self.

28

PLUM BLOSSOMS *FOR KATAGIRI-ROSHI*

Because it is withered, or bent and gnarled, all at once a plum tree blossoms: one, two, three, four, five. Isn't it the same for us? Isn't it true that through this same kind of condition we flower?

THE LATE DAININ KATAGIRI-ROSHI was the founder and abbot of the Minnesota Zen Center. The last talk and poem he gave to his *sangha* was Plum Blossom. (Coincidentally, just before his funeral Shinko and I had the chance to visit his temple, where I gave a talk on plum blossoms.) The poem Katagiri-roshi offered was recorded by Dogen and was written by his teacher, Tendo Nyojo. The temple where Tendo Nyojo taught, and where Dogen studied in China, is on a peninsula across the large bay just south of Shanghai. It's a very large temple containing hundreds of rooms and buildings. Overall, the Communist Chinese government has not allowed practice to take place in this temple, but since 1978, when the monks and nuns were allowed to return to the temple, the practice slowly has been reestablishing itself. The Chinese name of the temple is Tian Tong, which means "Heavenly Lad Temple."

There is a story behind this temple's name dating back to C.E. 304. According to the story, the monk Giko wanted to build a temple, but the task was far too great; he had no money, no food, and no supplies. The monk lacked absolutely everything needed to accomplish his goal, except his great vow. One day a young lad suddenly appeared to help this monk, and the two of them began building the temple together. After the large temple was completed, the young lad told the monk that it was time for him to leave. The monk asked him where he would go. The boy told him that he had been sent by order of the Heavenly King to help the monk establish the temple, and now that this was done, it was time for him to return. I don't know what you make of this story, but it's been almost eight hundred years since the temple was completed, and in addition to Dogen, many monks have practiced the Buddhadharma there over the centuries. At the same time Tian Tong has also endured many disasters to this day.

In *Moon in a Dewdrop,* Kazuaki Tanahashi's collection of Dogen's writings, he gives us this translation of the poem Katagiri-roshi used for his Dharma talk not long before he died. We should note that traditionally the plum blossom is used as a Zen metaphor. In this case, notice that the naturally severe condition of cold frost and snow furthers its blossoming:

> *Tian Tong's first phrase of midwinter.*
> *Old plum tree bent and gnarled.*
> *All at once, opens one blossom,*
> *two blossoms, three, four, five blossoms.*
> *Uncountable blossoms. Not proud of their purity,*
> *Not proud of fragrance.*
> *Spreading, becoming spring.*
> *Blowing over grass and trees,*
> *balding the head of a patch-robed monk.*

Whirling, changing into wind,
wild rain, falling snow, all over the earth.
The old plum tree is boundless.
A hard cold rubs the nostrils.

This is a very powerful and beautiful poem. One way for us to understand the condition expressed by the line "Old plum tree bent and gnarled" is that it is withered, aged, and useless. This is actually a Zen phrase expressing the condition where there seems to be no life. But this "no life" is exactly where life comes from. Because it is withered, or bent and gnarled, all at once a plum tree blossoms: one, two, three, four, five. Isn't it the same for us? Isn't it true that through this same kind of condition we flower?

In the Zen marriage ceremony the priest reads three statements, one of which says, "Life is without excitement. Life is completely still, regardless of whether it is dramatic or not." The background of life is always old and ancient, completely still; this is what we mean by "bent and gnarled." It may seem almost inhuman, but actually this seemingly sad and alone-feeling phrase expresses the very essence of being human. We should try not to apply our usual ideas and understandings to these kinds of expressions. For example, another phrase many people who have read about Zen have come across is "The wooden man sings and dances, and the stone woman gives birth in the night." These phrases express the same condition as "withered, bent, and gnarled." *Completely still* is the essence of each of them.

Of course, this is very difficult to explain, but even if you can't grasp it with your intellectual mind, and even if my explanation is not very good, you already have it. *Bent* means that like the tree, we don't stand up straight. The tree, and the *treeness* of the tree, have withstood all kinds of conditions and hardships, all kinds of weather. Yet the tree doesn't move, it just stands there actively accepting "the wind, the wild rain, the snow" as the various conditions of its natural life. But even so, no matter what the conditions or the experiences of its life may be, complete stillness meets it face to face.

Our lives are very much the same as the old plum tree. If we understand some of the background of the plum tree, our human life can gain great meaning. Laughing and crying, sadness, betrayal, sickness, or maybe joyfulness, dignity, love and strength, all of these are human examples of what the poem means by "wind, wild rain, snow." One thing follows another, changing, changing, changing without end. Some people may read this poem and say that the tree was betrayed by the wind or the snow. But how can a tree be betrayed? So we have to learn from this tree: How does it do it? How does it stand there in the midst of the conditions it survives and still give off blossoms? How can we do this in our lives?

"Old plum tree, bent and gnarled." It sounds almost pitiful, but through this condition, all at once open one blossom, two blossoms, three. These blossoms are us, four, five, six, seven, until they become immeasurable, uncountable blossoms. And being fully opened, we are not proud of our purity, or what we've learned, what we've experienced. We are not arrogant about any spiritual achievement. Nor are we proud of our fragrance, which is none other than the sweet fragrance of plum blossoms. We are not even conscious of our own fragrance. We need not be conscious of our own fragrance because we don't measure or judge ourselves at all.

As this manifesting continues, always changing, one minute appearing, disappearing the next, it is "spreading, becoming spring." Just one plum blossom means spring. I'm always amazed on Sonoma Mountain. Very early, every year without fail, though according to the calendar it's not yet spring, first the mimosa blooms, and after the mimosa the plum blossoms begin to appear. Within small crevices of this mountain, brilliant plum blossoms are blooming. For whom? In the valley, even beside the railroad track, a brilliant plum blossom is blooming. For whom? Within the environment of the tree, *bent and gnarled,* the condition is exactly right. This is "becoming spring."

There is spring in winter, and there is spring in autumn. There is spring in summer; there is also spring within spring. This is beyond mere human speculation, and because of it the blossoms blow over grasses, the most humble of things, and they blow over the tops of redwood trees. Small as they are, they bald the heads of patch-robed monks, shaving them, inspiring and renewing their life-force. They even actually become patch-robed monks. The petals of falling plum blossoms look like snow covering the whole earth. The old plum tree is boundless; it reaches everywhere, it touches everything, including you and me.

The last line of the poem is "A hard cold rubs the nostrils." Traditionally, when we dedicate statues of buddhas and shrines, there's a ceremony in which we paint in the eyes. This painting of the eyes gives life to the statues and structures. When we dedicated the stupa for Suzuki-roshi, his son, Hoitsu-roshi, stood in front of the large Tassajara stone and, with his hand holding a brush moving through the air, painted in the eyes with his unmoving presence. This last phrase, "A hard cold rubs the nostrils," is like the painting of the eyes of the statue. This ignites the poem, and the whole thing becomes alive. When this poem was written, there were three feet of snow on the ground at Tian Tong, so when Dogen writes, "A hard cold rubs the nostrils," that's really cold. Cold like that can ignite the poem, but it can also ignite the life of the plum blossoms as well as you and me.

This is the boundlessness of the old plum tree, its limitless ability to transform. In the text for this poem Dogen wrote:

> The old plum tree is boundless. All at once, it blossoms, opens, and of itself, the fruit is born. . . . It makes spring. It makes winter. It arouses wind and wild rain. It is the head of a patch-robed monk. It is the eyeball of an ancient Buddha. It becomes grass and trees. It becomes pure fragrance. Its whirling, miraculous transformation has no limit. . . . When the old plum tree suddenly opens, the whole world blossoms. . . . Blossoming is the old plum tree's offering.
>
> The old plum tree is within the human world and the heavenly world. The old plum tree manifests both human and heavenly worlds in its treeness. Therefore, hundreds and thousands of blossoms are called both human and heavenly blossoms. Myriads and billions of blossoms are Buddha-ancestor blossoms. In such a moment, "All the Buddhas have appeared in the world," is proclaimed. "The Buddha-ancestor was originally in this land," is proclaimed.

From the time the Buddha came into the world until now, approximately ninety-one generations have passed. It is a bridge nearly twenty-six hundred years long. Through the whole lineage, through all time, what is transmitted is this blossom. The old plum blossom is the meaning of this entire transmission from generation to generation. I hope you will remember this: "The Buddha-ancestor was originally in this land." A tree does not move around. It does not go from place to place. It stands still. And therefore it blossoms.

29

THE WORDLESS
PROCLAMATION

When you become familiar with returning your radiance
inward to your pervasive awareness and cultivate just this
as your life-force, you can return and cultivate it
anywhere. No matter where you are or what is going on,
you can "fix" or "turn on" your mind.

SOMEONE ONCE ASKED a Zen master, "How old is Buddha?" The Zen master replied, "How old are you?" This is good Dharma. To help us to remember and to realize this, every year in April we have a celebration for the birth of the Buddha. The Dharma, or truth, expressed by this ceremony is very profound. As the entire *sangha* and all of our guests intone a primordial chant, one by one we approach the shrine where a small figurine of the Buddha is standing in wordless proclamation with one hand pointing toward the earth and the other hand pointing toward heaven. This sign of the Buddha's birth is asking that the vastness of heaven and earth recognize and acknowledge the very vastness within each of us since the original minds of human beings and buddhas are exactly the same. Then, with acknowledgment and reverence, we bathe the baby Buddha by pouring a portion of sweet tea over its crown. This sweet tea is reminiscent of the sweet, misty fragrance of gentle rain that descended upon the garden of Lumbini where the Buddha was born, and each person has an opportunity to offer it in their own way. But we should ask ourselves, Who is being bathed by this act? Who is being acknowledged? It is certainly not something outside ourselves. Again, the vastness of the Buddha's birth is our very own vastness, and so the Buddha's wordless proclamation is that you yourself, standing between heaven and earth, are Buddha, and the physical gesture of pouring sweet tea recognizes and reminds us of this truth.

The significance of the small Buddha standing there alone under the shrine canopy, receiving the offering of sweet tea from each person, is very important for us to understand because it points to another fact: that ultimately there is nothing we can rely on. Remember, it is said that Shakyamuni Buddha's last words were: You are the light. We want to rely on something or somebody—our family, our car, our computer. But just like the Buddha's birth, each of us stands alone, and as you must remember, the body we have is with us for only a limited period of time. It's on loan, a kind of rental body. In our everyday life it's pretty common for someone to ask, "Do you rent, do you lease, or do you own?" When it comes to these bodies, these minds, and these lives, we don't do any of the three. But when we really know that we don't, then we realize that we do and that the time we have with this body is very limited; so life becomes very precious.

It's an established fact in the Buddhadharma that this body is not ourselves. In Dharma teachings all human beings are made up of five clusters or groups, known by the Sanskrit word *skandhas*. These *skandhas* include form, sensation, perception, discriminating thought or activity of the mind, and consciousness. In the Heart Sutra we chant that the five *skandhas* that compose human beings are all empty. The word *emptiness* is very important for those who practice the Dharma or simply seek the truth. When you first hear this word, it may sound negative, but it truly describes the fullness of your mind whose spacious nature is ready to receive. *Emptiness* is the same as *no-mind,* but when you use the phrase *no-mind,* it can be misunderstood quite easily because we do have a mind. But both *no-mind* and *empty mind* could refer to something like an empty bottle. We say that the bottle is empty of any content, and yet there is the bottle before us. *Only* when it is empty can it receive and be filled.

As we continue to live our lives, it's very difficult to receive something because more and more we fill ourselves with everything else, often searching to find something, anything, to rely on. But first we must return to zero so we can receive. Emptiness in this sense is very important. We especially need to be empty of our idea of ourselves, of who we think we are. Who we think we are is not who we are. This practice, and *zazen,* is the vehicle that helps us to express this inconceivable, wondrous fact. Once we do realize it, we also realize the other side: Who else could this wondrous condition be but ourselves? This self is filled with awareness and wisdom-knowing, accompanied by compassion.

I find it interesting that in Europe and America scientists have been using atom smashers to discover what is behind even the most infinitesimal elements of matter. What is behind, behind, behind? This is the big question that has inspired religion, philosophy, and science alike. Basically, when the scientists complete their exploration, their conclusion will be what the Buddha also realized almost twenty-six hundred years ago: emptiness.

Empty of the self, yet filled with bright awareness. I suppose the difference may be that the scientists will then have the theory and recipe, but they may not be interested in eating the meal.

There is a cathedral that was built in the eleventh century in Kraków, the ancient capital of Poland, called the Wawel Cathedral. I had heard about the Wawel many times because it is supposed to be one of the powerful energy spots or *chakras* of the earth. We had a rare opportunity to visit, and when we got there, we were allowed to go below the altar underneath the cathedral. I don't know exactly what I was expecting to encounter, but when I arrived, there was a deep quiet and calm presence, a truly pervasive sense of peace. It was so calm and peaceful that I felt as if I were being embraced.

This is the same as your mind. We say we are a cerebral brain or mind, but that mind is not us by far. Your body is not yours; your mind is not yours; therefore you may not be who you think you are. This is the exact opposite of what we are told every day in our society. But in the Dharma, instead of looking outside for everything, you look inside through the practice, while you begin to trace and return sights and sounds back to their origin. When you try to locate this mind, you'll discover that there is nothing there. Eventually you will arrive within yourself at the same pervasive peacefulness that I encountered at the Wawel Cathedral. There is a term Zen master Bankei used to describe this place that I like very much: *the unborn*. When you become aware of this *unborn,* you will see that Bankei's great compassion in leaving this term is the same original mind as yours.

Living words like *the unborn* help us to see things we've studied over and over again but from another angle. It's like seeing Sonoma Mountain from a different view; it is the same mountain you've seen many times, but you see it from its many perspectives. I recall first seeing Mount Fuji in Japan. From the tourist side it looks perfect, the mountain is very symmetrical with the snowcap on top, but one time I was behind the mountain, and it was quite different. It was not the "postcard Fuji" but asymmetrical and somehow more alive, with its own unique beauty. At the time I thought I was looking at Mount Fuji, but now I realize I was actually looking at myself.

When words are living words, like *the unborn* and *standing alone,* they can act just like this view from the other side and provide many insights for us. For instance, Buddha's second noble truth is that we suffer in life because we think everything is fixed and permanent. But the truth of life is that everything is in constant change, impermanent, full of the energy of life, and, ultimately we face it alone. We can't rely on anything. But actually this is our saving grace.

One time when Zen master Seung Sahn asked his student a question, the student answered, "One." Seung Sahn said to the student, "Where does this 'One' return to?" Even the One has to return somewhere. The student replied, "I don't know." Seung Sahn smiled at her and said, "Only don't know—wonderful!" It's the same with *the unborn*; you can't define it, you can't grasp it, but it is to be realized. We long for this.

The birth of the Buddha is about the proclamation of *the unborn.* If it's unborn, it means it can't die, because it never was created. When the temporal body of a great teacher dies, there is still this eternal life that continues aeon after aeon, or *kalpa* after *kalpa,* beyond space and time. Realized or not, this is the case because there is no beginning and no end. It is the same when ordinary people die; there is the same eternal life because eternal life *is* the *no-mind,* or *unborn,* this infinite spaciousness and great peace that we cannot define because it is not limited

by any conditions. Some of you may have experienced this by being with those who have died. It is neither here nor there, big nor small, female nor male, neither living nor dead. It's beyond words. That's what it means to be a wordless proclamation. We can't say anything about it. But that's also why it's great. (*Great* means "no beginning, no end.") We should know that we are inherently endowed with this greatness. This is what the proclamation of the birth of Buddha is all about. Real practice is the realization of this. That's our celebration.

When you bathe the Buddha during the ceremony, you are really bathing yourself as an acknowledgment of *the unborn* within and without you. *The unborn* is your original self nature, your original mind. Only in this way is there eternal life. From *the unborn* there is the birth of the Buddha. And the Buddha's birth is the celebration of your *unborn*ness. No creation, no destruction, no process of realization, no Zen, no Buddha. Just complete affirmation. And as I've said earlier, the fact that not one word can be said about it is what makes it great.

It takes some kind of attention or focus, which we call *samadhi,* for a person to turn their light inward so that they may enter the space of *the unborn. Samadhi's* function is the light or soft focus on this *unborn* space. And just as at Wawel, your experience of being there may also be this pervasive sense of peace. This spaciousness is the origin from which all energy emerges and to which it returns. Awareness of *the unborn* is the characteristic of *prajna. Prajna* is your intrinsic wisdom, innately bright. We say that in *samadhi* there is *prajna* and in *prajna* there is *samadhi.* They go together like two wings of a bird that knows the essence of soaring through and through. *Samadhi* is the focus on the essence of original mind. *Prajna* is the active awareness of that pervasiveness. *Samadhi* is the unwavering attention needed to touch *the unborn,* and *prajna* is the awareness of that essence. *Samadhi* is calm and quiet yet aware. *Prajna* is aware yet calm and quiet. *Samadhi* is *samadhi* and *prajna* is *prajna.* The essence of meditation practice is both *samadhi* and *prajna.* We are two very good, longtime friends.

Even though you may practice and cultivate *samadhi* and love sitting in *samadhi* so much that you do not want to leave it, you cannot just remain there. Sticking in *samadhi* is being stuck. You have to activate the *samadhi,* and this is the functioning of *prajna.* The spaciousness that characterizes *samadhi* is not a matter of conscious knowing; it is the equanimity of the "don't know" mind. As you become more and more able to return to this "don't know" mind (which is another name for *the unborn,* or emptiness, or self nature, or original mind) during *zazen,* you will find that you can begin functioning with it in your nonmeditation hours as well. For example, you will discover that you are not in the kind of hurry you've been used to, and there will be a spaciousness in your work. There will be energy, curiosity, zest, humor, and joy. And there will also be a certain newness to everything because your living is an expression of *the unborn*. Even if it appears that what you are doing is the same old thing, you will find that it is new; you can see and appreciate the flowers on the roadside even as you just drive by. With spacious awareness as its foundation, this is the way that *prajna* functions in your daily life.

Remember, the center of a moving cyclone is still. You are not in a hurry, but things still get accomplished. It's not like you will suddenly start walking slowly or thinking slowly, but you will find that things are actually being accomplished and that they are getting done right on time by themselves. "We" are doing less. *Nondoing* is a good word for this. In this way absolute time is relative time. There's no need to be in a hurry, though if you are in a hurry, you should be aware that you're in a hurry, and you should hurry one hundred percent. When you "only hurry," it's no hurry at all. It's the same as "only sit." Only sit, only hurry. It's quite different and not at all the struggle of the dualistic hurry. It's only hurry *as it is*. Real practice enables us to live in this way.

When you become familiar with returning your radiance inward to your pervasive awareness and cultivate just this as your life-force, you can return and cultivate it anywhere. No matter where you are or what is going on, you can "fix" or "turn on" your mind. This phrase comes directly from my own experience with my teacher. In the early days Suzuki-roshi urged me to "fix my mind." That's what he said. After all these seasons I am now understanding that what he was urging me to do was to maintain my focus on this pervasive awareness everywhere, not only during *zazen*. He was encouraging me to regain the imperturbable composure in whatever I did so that I could be free.

This is one of the reasons I encourage you to maintain real practice. You will discover from your personal experience that there is great joy and gratitude when your practice has a stable foundation. Little by little you will begin to realize that these teachings are actually true; that the precious Dharma manifested and expressed is always with you. Of course, it's paradoxical that in Zen you can't say what this *unborn* is, and yet there are a multitude of Zen texts written about it. In all the sutras and Dharmas, each and every volume upon volume is directly pointing to "you." But eventually you will realize the truth behind the living words. You will come to know without doubt that it is *the unborn* because it was never created. And since it was never created, it's beyond any conditions; it does not change. We can say, in a way, it is permanent and real. Therefore this is the only *stuff* we all can rely on.

30

TURNING YOUR
RADIANCE INWARD

*If clouds were to appear in the sky, it would hardly disturb
anything, just as many waves appearing in the ocean
would hardly be disturbing. They are the very life-activities
of sky / ocean. The beginningless space, the unlimited azure
sky / ocean—emptiness, by which I mean unconstricted,
pure, natural awareness—effortlessly absorbs them all.
This is your mind, the essence of your self-nature without
limitation, no beginning, no end. This is the radiance of
your original mind.*

THIS MORNING a very small finch visited my window and sang some truly beautiful songs. This is nature's
way of *just doing*, or *nondoing*, without the sense of self.
The finch was so small, I found it a bit surprising that, in spite of
its size, it was able to express such a brilliant and moving song.
Again and again it sang, each song differently, until it decided to
fly away. It wasn't the duration of the singing that so touched me,
it was just how it sang: The finch became its song. Without thinking at all, its expression came directly from its life-force. Isn't
this what we long to do in our lives? To find a way for our essence

to be expressed? I feel that all human beings unknowingly want, or long, to do this very thing. In fact, though they are not aware of it, I believe this is one of the deepest wishes of human beings the world over.

It's been windy lately, and quite a few people here at the temple and down in the valley have been saying it's been a little too windy. But it's spring, and the wind's nature blows and matures things as it moves them about. Pollen and seeds are being spread in the air; that's how nature works. It's just like the singing of the finch. If we stop the wind from moving, which we do in our minds, we do so just to our personal advantage. We don't take the big picture into account. Maybe we are motivated by the discomfort we feel from allergies. Still, it's not to the harmony of the whole. When we see the world with this dualistic orientation, it is neither good for us nor the whole. In fact, it may create a great amount of conflict in our lives.

This theme reminds me of a six-line poem that Suzuki-roshi loved. It was written in the ninth century by Tozan-zenji, who you could say is one of the founders of our Soto school. Apparently Tozan had experienced some kind of realization during a dialogue he had with his teacher, Ungan Donjo Daiosho. But he still had some doubts. After their dialogue Tozan left the monastery and began walking through the countryside until he came upon a stream. As he was crossing the stream, he saw his reflection in the water, and suddenly all of Tozan's troubles and doubts regarding his question of life and death were clearly washed away. Can you imagine that? All of your doubts, troubles, and worries washed away for good? All of your "allergies"?

In the spring of 1970 Roshi asked me to give the Saturday talk at Zen Center. I have to say I felt relieved when he changed his mind, but I also feel fortunate because, after his *teisho,* he handed me Tozan's poem written out in Roshi's own hand. This is Suzuki-roshi's translation of the six-line poem that expresses Tozan's realization:

> *Do not try to see the objective world.*
> *You which is given as an object to see is quite different*
> *   from you yourself.*
> *I am going my own way and I meet myself which includes*
> *   everything I meet.*
> *I am not something which I can see (as an object).*
> *When you understand self which includes everything,*
> *You have your true way.*

This poem was written more than one thousand years ago, and yet it is still relevant to us because it expresses Dharma, which is beyond space and time. In our everyday world we tend to see things as literally apart from ourselves. Naturally you will see things in this way because your education and conditioning have a powerful effect on your experience of subject and object. Most people's relationship to subject and object may seem to be a fixed, seemingly solid thing: Subject is just here, object is over there. Through ignorance we have been taught to experience reality in this way from birth. But as long as this orientation maintains itself, as long as you think and live dualistically, you are actually separated from reality, and as a result, you suffer. Your realization comes when you see the objective world and realize that it is part of you: the birds singing, the trees, the mountains, the wind, the sky. It's all part of you. This is one realization of truth: You as subject realizes that the object is no other than you. It's so beautiful.

In meditation you are turning your radiance inward. Since we

切に為む他に従って覚ひることを

遅遅として我と疎なり

われ今独り自ら往く

処々渠に逢ふことを得ん

我今これ渠にあらず

応に須く与麼に会して

方に始めて如々に契ふべし

Do not try to see objective
world
You which is given as an
object to see
is quite different from
you yourself.

I am going my own way
and I meet myself
which inclonde every-
thing I meet.

I am not someting which I can
see (as an object)

when your understand self which inclonde everything you have your true way.

try not to see the objective world, there's only one whole world, the wholeness, completely contained within yourself. This is the radiance. How can you perceive the sky if you are not part of the sky? How could you feel love if you aren't love? So it has been said that from morning to evening, whether seeing, hearing, laughing, crying, happy, or angry, ultimately the question is, *Who is this person?* This person is no other than our original mind, the Big Mind, functioning in these various ways.

This is expressed so beautifully in a famous Japanese *waka* attributed to Zen master Bankei:

> *As this mind is unborn and undying*
> *earth, water, fire and wood*
> *are its temporary dwelling*

This body is the physical self, and when the physical self dies, we cannot see, we cannot hear, our feet can't run, our hands can't grasp. But original mind is still here, and again original mind is the one that has been seeing, hearing, laughing, or crying all along. I know that you still don't believe me when I say this—no matter what the Dharma says, you find it difficult to believe—but why do you think this is? At least one reason, maybe the most important one, is that we approach the Dharma with our dualistic, conditioned thinking. But the Dharma is not just a subject to think about. It is something to directly experience that actualizes the natural radiance of our original mind. Over a period of nearly twenty-six hundred years Zen has cultivated many ways to help us to do just this.

In this regard, the word *noumenon* is important for us to understand. From the point of view of the Buddhadharma, the awakened truth, noumenon is "sourceless source." The reason it is called sourceless source is that it is the source of our original mind, of who we are. It is not called "sourceless" just to give it a provocative name, but we have to say something in the relative, so we say "sourceless source." If we just say "source," it seems to be some "thing," the source, and as soon as we hear that, we will automatically form an idea. But when we say "sourceless," where is it? What is it? It's beyond conceptualizing. Therefore it's something we can't grasp in our usual way of thinking, something we can't put our finger on. This is the unconditional world, noumenon, the space our *samadhi* focuses on in *zazen*.

People have defined *samadhi* as intense concentration or intense, one-pointed absorption. But you can also experience it

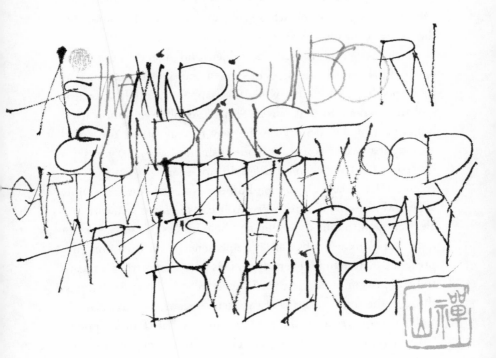

as a soft or light touch, as in resting. Each of these is a form of focus or attention. Human beings have all kinds of concentration: athletic concentration, surgeon's concentration, reader's concentration, lover's concentration, but Zen concentration, or *samadhi,* is to focus on the "sourceless source." *Samadhi* is like when you use a magnifying glass and want to burn a hole in a piece of paper. There are certain conditions necessary for this to occur. You have to hold the magnifying glass for a certain amount of time. You must hold it a certain distance from the paper, so there is space involved. Of course, there has to be sunlight. There has to be the piece of paper you want to burn, and you should hold the magnifying glass still; you can't move the magnifying glass and expect to burn the paper. This shows you a form of concentration or absorption where subject and object become one; this is the realization of truth.

Even though this is true, and subject and object become one, or you might say the oneness of subject and object is revealed as the paper begins to burn, when this happens in meditation it is still the scenery to realization. *Samadhi* is not realization itself but is part of the scenery on the way to realization. You could also say that when you sit on your cushion in *samadhi,* you are a "person of no concern"; things do not seem to disturb you. Nothing. Even *nothing nothing* bothers you. Yet you are vividly alive and present. If a fire were to break out, you're aware and alert enough to quickly get up and help others to safety. It's not a state of blankness, after all; it's a presence, your own immense presence that includes everything. This presence is what it means to be a "person of no concern." There are still thoughts that pass through the mind—this is always true because we are alive. As Keizan-zenji wrote in the last two lines of his famous poem, "Most people want to have pure clarity / But sweep as you will, you cannot empty the mind." Because the mind is already empty and yet filled with awareness, basically there is not much thinking. A thought is just one thought. Thinking is two thoughts. Thinking is thoughts connecting thoughts. But we are not thinking in *samadhi*. We are perfectly satisfied being where we are. No past, no future, even no present. Everything is complete. In fact, *zammai,* the Japanese word for *samadhi,* means "three times": past, present, and future. It is complete; it is beyond our intellect, our ego or dualistic mind. It's very difficult for the ego to function in this area because ego likes exclusiveness, limitation, distraction, and control, but *zammai* suggests the infinite, because your original mind is infinite and pervasive, undistracted and unconfined.

Another Japanese word for *samadhi* is *shoju. Ju* means "to receive," as in *jukai.* The ideogram is a hand above, a hand below, and a bar in the middle. It's giving and receiving and most often means "to receive." *Sho* means "right." But not right as opposed to wrong. It is something upright, of itself. It conveys that sense of rightness to it. The meaning of *shoju* is "upright, unhindered receiving of your own truth." This is another way to describe *samadhi.* We should ask ourselves, *Who is receiving? What is being received?*

Samadhi is a Sanskrit word that means "whole-together." Whole-together-completely. Of course, this is very good. It conveys a sense of dignity and decorum, poise, composure. Suzuki-roshi used to call it *imperturbable composure,* by which he meant the natural composure within yourself. This way of understanding who and what we are is not the "objective view," and it's a far cry from the you who you usually think you are in your daily life.

I find it interesting that in Webster's dictionary it says

noumenon is "the thing in itself." This refers to an object whose self is inaccessible to experience. Human beings experience things, but the most intimate thing is not-experiencing. This is the nondual, which means that the subject and object are identical. As long as you live as two things, subject *and* object, there's a separation between you and reality. That's why I repeatedly say you have to forget *this* self, the one who you think you are. Then you have the opportunity to discover *who this person is.*

Tozan-zenji's poem offers a pathway to answer this life-question right from the beginning. When he writes,

> *Do not try to see the objective world.*
> *You which is given as an object to see is quite different*
> *from you yourself.*

he is telling us we should not look outside, especially when we are practicing sitting. *Outside* could mean what is literally outside of your mind and body, but it can also mean all of the thoughts that are going on in your mind while you are sitting. I consider these thoughts "outside," too. They may be entertaining, of course, but because they are delusions, they are of no use to us. Following them when they appear only strengthens their apparent reality and our subject/object dualistic orientation. When they arise during our sitting, we should just be aware of them, nothing more. Our radiant awareness effortlessly and spontaneously causes them to vanish.

Tozan tells us we should avoid making an object of anything in the world, including ourselves. When you do try to see yourself "as an object to see," this separation limits your understanding and experience of who you are. Everything you encounter is considered something or someone "quite different from you yourself." This is a far cry from the vastness of original mind, the sourceless source, the noumenon, the thing in itself. And yet just before you see yourself as you look into a mirror, who else could it be but yourself? This seeming paradox is the double edge that gives and takes life.

People love to go to the ocean, but they may not fully understand why. I think we go because the ocean is *great* in the true sense of the word. It is *great* because it receives all rivers. It receives whatever waters flow into it without discrimination. Another way to say it is that it has no limitation; no beginning and no end. That's why people all around the world sit on the beach for hours enjoying it. Of course, this experience of limitlessness is not only found at the ocean; you may find it in the mountains, forest, or desert. And we should find it in *samadhi* during *zazen* where we are actually focusing on our original mind, calm and vast like the ocean or the sky.

If clouds were to appear in the sky, it would hardly disturb anything, just as many waves appearing in the ocean would hardly be disturbing. They are the very life-activities of sky/ocean. The beginningless space, the unlimited azure sky/ocean——*emptiness,* by which I mean unconstricted, pure, natural awareness—— effortlessly absorbs them all. This is your mind, the essence of your self-nature without limitation, no beginning, no end. This is the radiance of your original mind.

As Zen practitioners, we must know how to return to our natural inner radiance. Having a way to return to Big Mind, the mind without limitations, the mind that is everything but that at the same time is just your mind, is essential. The practice of *samadhi* makes a pathway for this return. Through your posture, your breath, your focus and concentration, you become aware of this infinite mind within yourself. When this awareness becomes stable within you, you no longer look at your hand and think, "That is my hand and those are my fingers," because that is seeing them as outside, as objects that are apart from you. They are part of your body just as the sky is part of your body. As Bodhidharma said, "The true body is the mind." This earth is part of your body, and all of these myriad things that constitute the universe are part of your body. We are, indeed, originally One. When you know this with your whole body and mind, it is a form of realization. And what is so wonderful is that each and every atom of the universe that comprises your whole body and mind has been given.

Tozan reminds us of this theme of giving when he writes, "You which is given as an object to see." The word *given* really leaps out for me. *You which is given*. Whether we are discussing various items in the *zendo* where we sit *zazen,* or large and small things in the world, we should know that it has all been given. Even this body was given. Whether we like this particular body or not doesn't matter; it was given and we received it. There is a saying: "Truly it is because the goodness of giving is inherent in oneself that one has now attained oneself." True giving is also the realization of the self, and the acts of giving and receiving come from this sourceless source, which is none other than your original mind.

Because of his realization Tozan was able to say, "Now I am going my own way." This *own way* includes everything. It is not the self-centered way but the universal way. Once we go this universal way, we can say with Tozan, "I meet myself which includes everything I meet." Do you understand? Once you are no longer separated from reality, once the duality of subject and object, inside and outside, appears less in your mind, you go your own way, this universal way, and you meet yourself everywhere, which includes everything you meet. It's like the birth of Buddha proclaiming "I alone am the world-honored One!" because wherever you go, and whatever you encounter, is you, originally One. *This* one! That's why Tozan tells us, "I am not something which I can see as an object," or as something outside of myself.

The next line of the poem is the compassion of wisdom because Tozan not only realized it himself but said it for us. He is really saying it as it is here, which is why this poem has been remembered for more than one thousand years:

> *When you understand self which includes everything,*
> *You have your true way.*

This *when* at the beginning of these lines marks the exact point in time and space where the awareness of this original mind manifests into wisdom and compassion. It's like the sound of my stick striking against the floor: *When!* That's the moment of your realization, and this realization is the entirety of Zen, revealing yourself and helping the many because they are also you.

During the early part of his life, before Hui Neng became the Sixth Ancestor, he was a woodcutter. Every day he would go to the forest where he would cut, gather, and carry enough firewood to sell in the marketplace. This is how he supported his mother and himself. One day while he was selling wood, a monk passed by chanting the Diamond Sutra. The phrase of the sutra that Hui Neng heard and that led to his enlightenment was "Do not dwell on anything that arises from the mind." The Diamond Sutra also proclaims that all compounded things are like a dream, a phantom, a bubble, or a reflection. They are like dew or lightning; they are entirely void of substance. We should really fathom this. Hui Neng couldn't read or write, so his realization was based on his natural *samadhi,* which was found within the simple and direct conditions of poverty in which he lived. When he heard the chant, he was already focused on the one-mind. The chant was like the straw that broke the camel's back, or the straw that *gave* the camel his back again, because Hui Neng's realization was through and through.

I want to emphasize the importance of not dwelling on or entertaining anything that arises in the mind. When you practice this "not dwelling," you are actually turning from the delusion of your dualistic thinking and returning to your sourceless source, the bright radiance and self-nature of your mind. Right there you have your true way. In practice we let go of the habit of dwelling on what arises in our minds, the impulses, conditions, and delusions that usually obstruct access to our original mind. We practice something different: how to *not* limit the expression of our true self, which is what occurs when we apply dualistic conditioning to the unconditional. It is clear that from within this empty, nondwelling space you are filled with radiant awareness, a pervasive quality with neither inside nor outside nor even in-between. It is your original mind, which has never left you for an instant.

Letting go of these habits of the dualistic mind requires that our awareness and focus are in accord. The Dharma repeats over and over again that when your awareness is aware of your dualistic thought, your thought will vanish. And it's true; our awareness is that radiant. Our practice makes it possible for us to return to our original mind-ground, which does not vanish, which cannot vanish, because it is real. Only delusions vanish.

In a Chinese sutra known as the Complete Enlightenment Sutra, there are several lines that again make this clear:

> *As this illusory body of sentient beings vanishes,*
> *This illusory mind also vanishes.*
> *As this illusory mind vanishes,*
> *Illusory sense objects also vanish.*
> *As illusory sense objects vanish,*
> *This illusory vanishing also vanishes.*
> *As this illusory vanishing vanishes,*
> *That which is not illusory does not vanish.*

Isn't that wonderful? That which is true does not vanish; only delusion vanishes. And it is our awareness of our delusions that makes them vanish effortlessly. *Poof! As it is!* Usually the truth is covered or obscured because our practice is not clear and strong, but "practice is like polishing a mirror until the brightness appears" means that the mirror is always there; even a small, clear portion will do. This brightness is the radiance of our original mirror-mind.

We can't just think about this and try to understand it and hope that someday it might happen. It does take real practice and direct experience to lead us to the point where we can begin to do this often and repeatedly. (But it doesn't take sitting for thirty years for it to happen, either. That idea is just the same old dualistic mindset that says, "If I do this, then *that* will happen.") What is required is for you to sit with imperturbable composure, sometimes soft and sometimes intense, with your mind in *samadhi:* one whole-together-completely. The more you practice and return to the sourceless source, the more you are naturally able to return. This is how to renew our lives moment after moment. This is what it means to say that life right now is infinite or eternal. You are returning to one, zero, or home, depending upon how you express emptiness. Whatever you call it, it *is* your most intimate home. The important point is that it is made possible by real practice. Only practice transforms the self that clings to obstacles—especially greed, anger, and ignorance—and obstructs access to your original mind.

There are many ways to practice returning home besides counting breaths, and as I've already mentioned, Breath Sweeps Mind is a good one, using the natural sound of the exhale to sweep away thoughts. When you practice it, you should continue sweeping even when there's no dust, sweeping away sweeping.

Another way to practice it would be to return to the origin of a sound. This is something we practiced together one morning, and it was a threshold experience for many people. We listened to the song of a bird, and instead of going outside, outside, as we usually do, we turned our radiance inward, and within a short period we arrived in the space of one mind. We followed the sound back to its origin, the sourceless source, and at that point there wasn't anything to grasp. We realized how vast and pervasive, how unbroken and uninterrupted that space is. And because its nature is like that, it is impossible to give it a name. We can't say whether it is large or small, near or far, coming or going. In the space of one mind, you can't hear the sound, you can't hear anything. You hear no-thing. It's the very meaning of the Zen saying "What is it that thus cometh?" This is seeing no-thing. Zen practice is also just this! When you practice it, you should be thoroughly familiar with this state, so you naturally return again and again. It's a matter of cultivating your awareness of your self-nature a hundred thousand times. All Zen practices lead to emptiness, our most intimate, real home.

This is the practice found in the Ten Ox-herding pictures: The ox pulls that way, and you pull this way; the ox pulls this way, and you pull that way. The ox always wants to go to greener pastures. Our function is simply to be aware first and gently pull it back. This dissolves our thinking as we return to the sound of the breath. Each step of this practice is done on the exhale.

If we are doing the practice I mentioned above, we follow the one sound as we go behind whatever appears, including other sounds, thoughts, feelings, and the like. No matter how many times we have to do this, our practice helps us to continue on. At the *sangha* house there's a *sumi* painting of an ox and its herder. The rope with which the ox herder is leading the ox is as fine as a thread. Initially, in order to control the ox, you try to pull with a strong rope, but with practice it turns into a thread. That's when your effort, concentration, and discipline have matured and become stable so that this familiarity with your self-nature, your one mind, can be turned on again and again. It seems like it goes where you go, and the truth is that it does. It is all-encompassing, ever-pervasive. It's the whole universe. Wherever you go, it is with you and has never left you for one instant. It is said that those whose hands and feet are moved by it are as numerous as the sand grains of the Ganges.

Appendix

Ten Characteristics of Our Inconceivably Wondrous Nature

The One-Mind Precepts of Bodhidharma

In the instruction, to receive is to transmit; to transmit is to awaken; and to awaken the Buddha Mind is called true *jukai*. Each precept is a vignette of the one-mind that is always with us.

1. Self-nature is inconceivably wondrous; in the everlasting Dharma, not raising the view of extinction is called "not killing."

2. Self-nature is inconceivably wondrous; in the ungraspable Dharma, not arousing the thought of gain is called "not stealing."

3. Self-nature is inconceivably wondrous; in the Dharma of nonattachment, not raising the view of attachment is called "not being greedy."

4. Self-nature is inconceivably wondrous; in the inexplicable Dharma, not expounding a word is called "not lying."

5. Self-nature is inconceivably wondrous; in the intrinsically pure Dharma, not arousing ignorance is called "not being intoxicated."

6. Self-nature is inconceivably wondrous; in the faultless Dharma, not talking about sins and mistakes is called "not talking about others' faults and errors."

7. Self-nature is inconceivably wondrous; in the Dharma of equality, not talking about self and others is called "not elevating oneself and putting down others."

8. Self-nature is inconceivably wondrous; in the genuine, all-pervading Dharma, not clinging to one single thing is called "not being stingy."

9. Self-nature is inconceivably wondrous; in the Dharma of no-self, not contriving a reality of self is called "not being angry."

10. Self-nature is inconceivably wondrous; in the Dharma of oneness, not raising a distinction between Buddhas and beings is called "not slandering the Three Treasures."

PERMISSIONS

THE AUTHOR GRATEFULLY acknowledges the following for permission to reprint quotations used herein:

Alan Schwartz, for use of his personal letter. John Stevens, for *Shobogenzo (The Eye and Treasury of the True Law),* published by Nakayama Shobo, translation © 1975 by Kosen Nishiyama and John Stevens. Taigen Daniel Leighton, for quotations from *Cultivating the Empty Field: The Silent Illumination of Zen Master Hongzhi* (expanded edition published by Tuttle Publishing, 2000). San Francisco Zen Center, for all published and previously unpublished material by Shunryu Suzuki-roshi. Zen Center of Los Angeles, for quotations from *The Record of Transmitting the Light,* Zen Master Keizan Denkoroku © 1991, and *The Way of Everyday Life: Zen Master Dogen's Genjo Koan with Commentary by Hakuyu Maezumi* © 1978. University of California Press, for *Branching Streams Flow in the Darkness: Zen Lectures on the Sandokai,* Shunryu Suzuki, edited by Michael Wenger, © 1999 San Francisco Zen Center, and *Dogen's Manuals of Zen Meditation* by Carl Bielefeldt, © 1988 the Regents of the University of California. University of Hawaii Press for *Shobogenzo,* by Thomas Cleary, © 1986, and *Korean Approach to Zen, The Collected Works of Chinul,* translated by Robert Buswell, © 1983. Reprinted by permission of North Point Press, a division of Farrar, Straus and Giroux: "Baika #1" from "Plum Blossoms" from *Moon in a Dewdrop* by Dogen, translated by Kazuaki Tanahashi, translation copyright © 1985 by the San Francisco Zen Center. Excerpt from *The Unborn: The Life and Teaching of Zen Master Bankei, 1622–1693*, translated by Norman Waddell, © 1984 by Norman Waddell. Excerpt of seven lines from *Selected Poems 1947–1995* by Allen Ginsberg, © 1996 by Allen Ginsberg. Reprinted by permission of HarperCollins Publishers Inc.

About the Author

JAKUSHO KWONG was born in Santa Rosa in 1935. He grew up in Palo Alto and after school worked in commercial art. In 1960 he began to study Zen with Shunryu Suzuki-roshi in San Francisco and was ordained in 1970. Two years after Suzuki-roshi died in 1971, he co-founded Sonoma Mountain Zen Center, as an expression of gratitude to his teacher and to continue the Soto practice lineage. Every week, from 1973 to 1978, he studied the transmission ceremony with the late Kobun Chino Otogawa-roshi. In 1978 he completed Dharma transmission through Hoitsu Suzuki-roshi under the supervision of Hakusan Noiri-roshi at Rinso-in temple in Japan, authorizing him as successor in Suzuki-roshi's lineage. In 1995 he completed further training and was given the title of Zen Teacher, *Dendo Kyoshi,* by the Soto School of Japan. He is one of nine Western Zen teachers to receive this acknowledgment.

He is the abbot of Sonoma Mountain Zen Center, where he lives with his wife, Shinko. Since 1986 he has visited and taught an international sangha in Iceland and Poland. He continues to teach Zen as nothing special but the aliveness we bring to each moment.